Fishing in Hong Kong

A How-To Guide to Making the Most of the Territory's Shores, Reservoirs and Surrounding Waters

by
Mike Sharp and John Peters

With illustrations by
Lizzie Sharp-Eliazar

Fishing in Hong Kong

ISBN 978-988-13764-8-0

Published by Blacksmith Books

Unit 26, 19/F, Block B, Wah Lok Industrial Centre, 37-41 Shan Mei Street, Fo Tan, Hong Kong

Tel: (+852) 2877 7899

www.blacksmithbooks.com

www.facebook.com/blacksmithbooks

The Locations

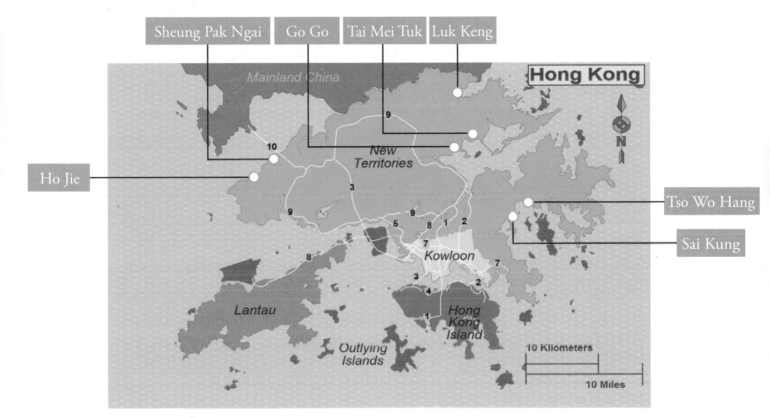

Contents

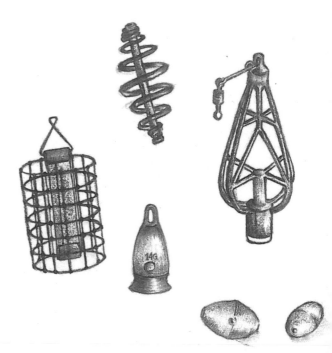

Introduction

It may seem strange to the Hong Kong reader that we have penned a book on angling in Hong Kong; one of the most cramped and overpopulated places in the world. However, if you live here for some time you may hanker for some of those hobbies and pursuits you followed in your own country. Expatriates befuddled about fishing in Hong Kong have often approached both myself and John about their failed trips to the many huge reservoirs situated around the territory or their frustrated attempts to fish off their boats.

So in order to assist the budding Hong Kong angler we have put this book together with the help of our fishing buddies coupled with the artistic talents of Lizzie, who has spent many hours sketching her way through our fishing boxes. Our aim is to point a beginner or dormant enthusiast in the right direction to get the most out of fishing the inland and coastal locations we have identified and trialled – and more importantly, to get them to catch fish!

By the time this book is published, some of the locations we have identified may have changed admission fees or productivity. We make no

View towards Tai Wan Village, Shan Liu and the Sai Kung Country Park in the background.

apologies for this as Hong Kong is a fast-moving environment and sometimes fishing businesses can be affected by the financial climate in much the same way as banks or retailers. Lakes and ponds may change in their recommended fishing style, the type of fish stocked or come under new management. Since this book was first written in 2014, the Tai Mei Tuk fishery has changed management and is currently not available to recreational anglers. We have decided to keep the chapter in the book for educational purposes as the methods described are useful elsewhere.

In respect of the techniques we recommend, these may be complemented by using other methods anglers have discovered in their home countries. There is no problem in this. If you have a new way to catch a particular species, we will be the first to ask you about it. In the end, we hope by reading this book, more people will be encouraged to take up angling, both in the local and expatriate communities, thereby promoting both conservation and the development of the sport within Hong Kong.

The
LOCATIONS

Tai Mei Tuk Fishing Farm
Tai Po

Tai Mei Tuk Fishing Farm is the largest and most organised commercial fishing lake in Hong Kong and is situated along the Ting Kok Road next to Plover Cove Reservoir Dam. The lake has been operating as a freshwater fishing venue for over fifteen years and has a large standing population of fish of which some have reached specimen size. The setting of the lake is beautiful with the Pat Sing Leng Mountain Range forming a backdrop. One half of the lake is surrounded by vegetation and there are numerous trees, which provide some shade from the sun. At its deepest, the lake can reach 4 metres depth however it averages at 2-3 metres with a pronounced shelf or drop-off going around about five metres from the bank where the bottom will slope down by a metre or so. Fishing is available from a reinforced bank bordering half of the lake and there are

pontoons placed over the lake so that anglers can fish directly over the deeper water and not crowd the banks.

It was a bright September day when myself, Lizzie and John arrived at the lake to experiment with a selection of fishing methods.

John had been talking about using the Chinese style whip-fishing method while I had already announced my intention to sticking to UK-style bottom-fishing in order to catch some of the bigger lake specimens. Lizzie had no intention to go fishing but would busy herself sketching the local fauna and providing encouragement or abuse depending on our angling performances.

Given that the lake is subdivided into three fishing areas, we decided to select a spot on

the larger section as it is well known to have specimen fish swimming around. John had opted to try the Chinese whip-fishing style and set up to my left approximately 10 metres away. This type of fishing normally consists of a 5-6-metre carbon-fibre pole with a length of line attached to it. The line will connect to a set of terminal tackle which has a thin float, weights and a double hook set up. The method is very accurate in that it is easy to repeatedly target the same point in the water with the float and thereby focusing your fishing to where the bait is landing on the bottom or mid-water.

However, you are limited in the size of fish you can safely land as you have a fixed line and it is easy to get broken up if a larger fish snatches the bait and swims away at speed.

Meanwhile, I stuck with my well tried UK-style bottom fishing set up, which consists of a 12 foot carp rod a bait runner reel and a method feeder at the end of the line. A 'bait-runner' is a reel that has a setting that allows a fish to pull line off the reel in a controlled manner when it swims off with the bait. You can hear a small buzz as the line leaves the

Mike with a Catfish landed by using a UK-style Carp landing net.

spool. Whereas a method-feeder is basically a small cage similar to a hair curler around which you can secure extra bait, and this settles around the hook-bait, when the tackle hits the water. As the fish investigate the pile of bait on the bottom, they will pick up the hook bait and run with it, thereby alerting the angler.

John was quickly set up and was float-fishing

Common Carp are frequently caught and a popular fish. UK anglers are fanatical about fishing for them, Aussies hate them and Chinese like to eat them with black bean sauce.

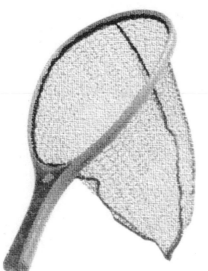

a spot directly to his front at about 2 metres depth. He had deliberately set his line a bit deeper so as the float would not drift with the surface wind. He was using a paste-mix and at the same time introducing some extra bait to his area to attract the fish. Each time he decided to re-cast, he would give the float a quick jerk so as to cause any remaining bait to fall off the hook and sit on the bottom in his fishing area (the 'swim'). I watched him out of the corner of my eye as I cast my lump of bait out to a reference point where the water reflection showed a distinctive pattern that I could remember. I tightened up my line and placed the rod in the rod rest and sat back to watch my fishing partner in action.

John was getting numerous bites and hitting fifty percent of them. From what I could see, most were Mud Carp with the odd Common Carp mixed in. He would lift the tip of his whip and set the hook and then his whip would bend into the fish as it dived around in the water in front of him. Now and then a larger fish of a kilo or so would come along and he would need to follow it around in the water with his limited fishing line until the fish became exhausted and surfaced.

I noticed my rod tip was bouncing up and down. This was a 'line bite' when a fish swims into the fishing line and is normally an indication that a fish is checking out the bait. I focused attention onto my reel and waited. There was a slight turn to the spool followed by a pause and then suddenly the spool started to turn confidently as the line shot out of the rod and cut a prominent 'V' across the water. A fish had taken my bait and was running and had detected the resistance of the hook and method feeder.

I turned the reel handle and clicked the drag in place and lifted the rod up at the same time thereby setting the hook. I immediately felt something of considerable weight shake its head and start to zig-zag across the lake. I started to pull back and wind the slack line however the fish would zoom off for another 10-metre dash. This lasted ten minutes and by then I managed to coax the fish into the water in front of me where it continued to dive and jerk around. By then I had realised I had a Catfish on the end as now and then, its ugly head would appear and it would shake its head and dive off again. Fighting a strong Catfish is similar to tackling a large eel with the snake-like movements around the pond, plus sudden changes in direction and an uncanny skill of snagging an angler on underwater obstacles. After charging around in front of me for another five minutes I was able to tire the fish out and bring it to the surface where Lizzie was able to slip the carp net underneath it.

Once a catfish is on the bank it is useful to have an old towel on hand to keep a grip of the fish while you unhook it, as it flips about and can slide out of your hands like a giant slug. Some anglers copy the 'hillbilly catfish noodlers' and grab the fish by its mouth and manoeuvre it around. I prefer to grab it behind its pectoral fins by using the friction of the towel to control it. In this case I was able to secure the fish and after weighing, found that I had caught a fourteen pounder. We took some photographs and then released it back into the lake to fight another day.

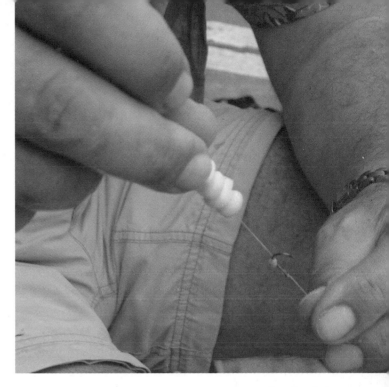

Hair-rigged sweetcorn. This is a method where bait is threaded onto a line attached to the hook.

John is using a 'bait catapult' to put extra bait into his swim. This is a skill that takes a bit of practice as 'misfires' can end with sweetcorn exploding all over the bank ... and angler.

I didn't get many more fish that day apart from a couple of four-pound common carp at the end of the session, so I went over to see how many fish John had amassed. My partner was grinning with a sort of self-satisfied look as he pulled out a full keep-net with over fifty fish in it. None were over three pounds, however anything bigger would have been very difficult to land with his whip, which cannot really give much line. However the method proved to be deadly as John's net full was evidence of.

So, before we stood the chance of facing traffic jams through Sai Kung, we packed up and paid our fees at the fishing hut. This was followed by a quick can of beer while we chatted about our days' catch and planned our next trip for the upcoming weekend.

fresh water bait

John with his net full of Common Carp, Mud Carp, Silver Carp and Tilapia. A haul reaching over 30 Kg of fish. All caught on sweetcorn float-fished on 10 pound line. No wonder he's smiling.

A late afternoon shot of local Hong Kong anglers at Tai Mei Tuk; fishing with whips and paste. In the summer, the umbrella is a must as the sun can get unbearable and anglers should cover up with long trousers and long sleeved shirts.

Notes - Tai Mei Tuk

Car Park and shop

(Beer and snacks)

Tai Mei Tuk Fish Farm

How to get there: Take the MTR to Tai Po Market Station and catch either the 75K Bus (slow) or the 20C green minibus. Green taxis available. Telephone number for TMT Office — 2662 6351.

Kit

Rods, reels, 8-10 pound line, stick floats, ledgers and feeders.
Split shot weights. Landing net, flask and sandwiches.

Bait

Sweetcorn, paste, bread (can be bought at shop there)

Hope to catch some carp (common, silver and mud), catfish, tilapia and gwai far.
BEER AVAILABLE!

Go Go Saltwater Pond
Tai Po

Go Go is a converted saltwater fish farm which offers saltwater fishing for a reasonable price. If you pay the full days fee you will be able to take home 3kg worth of your day's catch free of charge. Of course, if you catch more than that, you can expect to pay extra money but this is only fair after all, this is a business. This location is a well-stocked pond with large numbers of Pomfret, Red Drums and Barramundi. In addition there are Amberjacks, Rays, Mullet and several species of Snapper. Anglers can visit the pond all year round though I would not recommend fishing during periods of very cold weather or during the monsoon when large amounts of cold fresh water put the fish off feeding.

Mike setting up at Go Go.

Fishing methods

We have found two very effective methods with which to catch fish and you may try these or variants of these methods in your own visits. The first method entails a medium sized float or bung, a swivel, trace and a size 8 hook. A live prawn (one of the green estuarine species) is hooked through the tail and allowed to swim around pulling the float as it does. Predatory fish such as Barramundi will attack the prawn and you can generally see when this is going to happen as the prawn gets nervous and the float starts to be dragged around more erratically.

12

When the predatory fish grabs the prawn the float will disappear and the angler should stay calm and count to '5' to allow for the fish to consume the body of the prawn and thereby placing the hook in the best position to catch the fish's mouth. Following the strike, you will have a very exciting fight with a large fish between 3-7 Kgs and, in the event that you get him to the bank, a pair of pliers will come in handy in removing the hook from the nasty teeth these predatory fish carry.

A second very effective method is to visit a local fishing shop and purchase a block of frozen shrimp (krill) These are very cheap and you defrost them in a bucket of water at the lakeside. Once they start to defrost, you grab handfuls and throw them into your swim (the area where you will fish) in order to induce the fish to feed in your area. You then prepare a basic float fishing setup using a stick float, several shot and a size 10 hook and place 4-5 shrimps on the hook and cast out to your swim. Bites can either be gentle nervous types where the float totters about or quick and violent, with the float simply shooting away. On occasions the bigger fish will respond to this method so be careful when you strike as something bigger might be on the end.

It is important to position the hook on the bottom so that the bait sits naturally and the fish won't get suspicious. Bites are either fast or very light as the fish test out the bait. At the end of the day, you must remember to wash down your tackle in fresh water in order to prevent saltwater erosion that will quickly rot and corrode your equipment.

Bait-box fitted with an air pump that keeps the live-bait (prawns) alive while fishing. The motors are notorious for breaking down so the device should be maintained carefully.

One of Mike's Chinese floats with a prawn suspended below, waiting for a Barramundi or a 'Red'.

A good catch of Pomfret by Mike using krill float-fished.

salt water bait

Mike with a 7Kg Red Drum caught on a float fished live prawn and destined for the freezer.

John's Amberjacks caught on live prawn.

Mike (dehydrated) with a 6Kg Barramundi.

Freshly caught Asian Barramundi; similar to Australia's number one sporting fish and a popular 'eating fish'

John with his favourite hat – an important piece of kit for both Mike and John given that both are not blessed in the hair department.

Warning-The Rabbit Fish

Within the pond and other similar venues lies a very small fish carrying a very nasty weapon. It is called a Rabbit Fish and it can be found swimming along the side of ponds or along harbour walls. It is small and silvery to light brown in colour and has some black spines down its back. Should you have the misfortune of catching one, do not handle it with unprotected hands. Get a damp towel and hold the fish with the towel before removing the hook. The dorsal, pelvic and pectoral fins are the poisonous part and these should be avoided at all costs. John was stung by one of these before and describes the pain like a continual thumping on your head ...times 10. If you do get stung, you will survive but seek some medical help as the pain is excruciating.

Notes-Go Go

Go Go Fishing Notes

How to get there: If you go by car, watch out for the turning on the left. Public transport is the same as for Tai Mei Tuk, as the pond is along the Ting Kok Road.

Kit

Rods and reels, 10-15 pound line, stick floats and larger bung floats, 50 pound line for trace, weights, live bait (buy in wet-market) 10-4 hook sizes.

Bait

Need to buy some krill—frozen block, live green prawns and some sprats. Need live bait box with bubbler. (Check battery)

Hope to catch some Red Drums, mullet, snapper, barramundi, pomfret and grouper.

Need to take some fish home for bbq.

Luk Keng Saltwater Pond

We had heard about the Luk Keng Saltwater Ponds through our Latvian contributor, Alex, who works locally in the New Territories. He described it as having 'very clear water and holding loads of fish'. So both myself and John decided to take a Friday off and head up to the ponds, which are near Sha Tau Kok.

The journey to the ponds is quite attractive when coming from Tai Po as you head up the Ting Kok Road to Plover Cove Reservoir and pass along the side of the reservoir. The ponds lie to the left of a very straight piece of road, which has its own speed camera due to the popularity of joyriding in this part of the New Territories. The first thing you notice about the ponds is that the pool next to the owner's shop is very clear and you can see many nice fish swimming around. The other two ponds are brown in colour with visibility limited to about a foot. On this particular day, we noticed that there were many anglers positioned around the clear water pond presumably because it gave them more confidence by seeing the fish. So we moved to the long pool next to it and set up with one rod with live prawn and a second rod float- fishing

the frozen shrimp. It was a nice cool day and overcast which is ideal conditions for fishing. After three hours of fishing, I had caught two Pomfret and John had none.

The clear pond at Luk Keng where you can see your 'target fish' swimming around. This is both exciting and frustrating.

18

I could see he was getting frustrated, especially when he saw a pair of Amberjacks checking out the Pomfret I had put in the keep net.

Not wishing to see my partner get more miserable I suggested we hopped over to the clear water pond and try there. John stayed with his frozen shrimps on the float while I decided to have a go at lure fishing with a small rubber fish I had found in my tackle box. I could see a Grouper in the weed below me so I gently teased the rubber fish past him. He couldn't resist it and turned and snatched at the lure with his oversized mouth and I was into fighting an angry five pound grouper. John came over with the net and five minutes later I had the fish on the bank ready to be popped into the keep net. John was not too impressed and began to focus on his own fishing with renewed intensity. He continued to feed the frozen shrimp into his swim and noticed that something was removing his bait from the hook and he wasn't seeing the bite.

I sat with him and watched him and attempted to see into the water with my Polaroids. I couldn't see into the deep water where his bait was, however this didn't matter as John had seen a slight movement on his float. He leant forward and tightened up the slack line and when the float moved again he struck. At this point, his reel screeched as line was dragged out by the diving fish. His rod bent double and a powerhouse of a fish darted about and jerked with incredible force causing him to stand up to absorb the shocks in the rod. We couldn't see it at first and the fish fought hard and fast however after about five minutes it began to tire and John was able to bring it to the surface where

it jumped once and made one last dash for the bottom only to be brought back to the surface gasping. It was a beautiful Amberjack which is a member if the Tuna family and can be recognised by the black flash across its eyes. It is very popular with anglers as it tastes very good either as sashimi or cooked.

Following that catch we packed up and paid the old man looking after the place so that we could take some fish home. He charged quite a bit for this so whereas the cost of the fishing ticket was quite cheap, the removal of a fish became quite expensive. However we didn't mind as Pomfrets and Amberjacks are good eating.

During our day at the water, we noticed three methods in use by anglers present. The first method was float-fished 'krill' (small shrimps) with plenty thrown in around the float to encourage the fish to feed. The second method was live or dead prawn on a float and the third method was simply spinning either on the surface or just below the surface.

The venue gets busy on weekends and it is better to visit midweek if you have the chance. We saw some big Cobias swimming around as well as the usual Red Drum, Pomfret and Snapper. Grouper were keeping hidden away on the bottom. Since this chapter was written, we have returned to the water and found it still active and receiving regular re-stocking particularly with Pomfret.

Ragworm - an effective bait if properly secured to the hook. Anglers need to watch out for their pincers.

Red Drum caught on float-fished shrimp.
Note the distinctive black spot on the tail.

Luk Keng Village while looking in a north easterly direction across a disused
pond towards Sha Tau Kok and the border area. There is still barbed-wire left
on the nearby hill from the cultural revolution time.

Notes–Luk Keng Saltwater Ponds

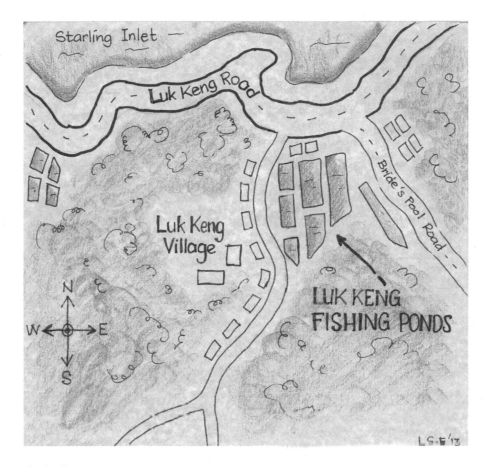

You can get there by car, driving along Bride's Pool Road from Tai Mei Tuk; or go to Fanling MTR and catch the 56K minibus from outside the station.

Need to take

Rods & Reels, 10-15 pound line, stick floats and bungs, weights, spinners and plugs, 50 pound trace, live bait box if taking live bait.

Hope to catch: reds, cobia, Pomfret. Amberjack, barramundi and grouper.

Need to take sandwiches and a flask of tea.

Beer available from the owners' fridge.

Toilet is clean.

Busy on weekends, especially on the clear pond.
Alex reckons the krill is best.

Sheung Pak Nai

South of Lau Fau Shan lies a quiet area of the New Territories, an area of lychee orchards, market gardens, and salt or freshwater fishponds. There are several notable fisheries and we shall focus on two; a freshwater pond at Sheung Pak Nai and a saltwater pond at Ha Pak Nai called Ho Jie.

Both myself and John have made a couple of visits to the freshwater pond and on both occasions filled our keepnets with Silver or Mud Carp and Tilapia. There are bigger fish about, however we have yet to catch any of these and it is recommended that a dusk to dawn session would result in a better catch. When it comes to big fish, we have generally looked at some of the other waters to satisfy our big fish ambitions.

In order to get there; if using public transport it is best if you alight at the Tin Shui Wai MTR Station and look for a taxi at Exit C1. A green New Territories taxi will charge about HK$50-60 to take you south of Lau Fau Shan along the Nim Wan Road and drop you at the pond, which comes up on the right, after a prominent 'modern-style' public toilet. You will see a scruffy-looking pond with platforms installed all of the way round and bright umbrellas advertising cigarettes

and beer. There is a large shed with a kitchen inside and a sort of makeshift café available. Toilets, bait and nets are available however, you should examine any loaned keepnets carefully as during my first visit, all of my fish made a 'great escape' out of a large hole near the base of my net… much to everyone's amusement.

Carp/Goldfish hybrid caused by aquarium owners introducing pet fish into local ponds where they cross breed.

The local Chinese like to fish with a whip, float and two hooks along with their own brand of paste. Both John and myself have stayed with the reliable sweet corn and managed okay on a standard float rig. Once the fish are fed some ground bait they seem to hang around the area in front of the angler and it is pretty straightforward to catch them. What is hard is trying to find a large fish and even though I have placed out large baits on the bottom of the pond, they have been gobbled up by smaller fish that have subsequently hooked themselves on my strong tackle. There are large Catfish and Common Carp within the pond, but trying to catch them requires a lot more focus and time. I have heard of anglers staying all night in order to maximise their time for the best fishing times at dusk and dawn.

During one of our visits to the pond, we became bored with catching Mud Carp and saw that the fishing shop was selling buckets of bread crust. John decided to experiment and threw a handful of crust onto the surface of the pond. The fish; mainly Tilapia, became very excited and started to rise and gobble down the crust. We changed our tackle to short stick floats with lead shot placed directly under the float. We left about 40cm of line between the float and the hook and fastened a piece of crust onto hook. We then cast out and pulled the float gently so that the line was straight between the float and the crust. When a fish took the piece of crust with the hook in it, we waited till the float moved off and struck. This proved to be a very effective way to catch the Tilapia and some were up to three pounds in weight. So by the end of the day, we had landed over thirty fish each which was a satisfying end to the trip.

Mud Carp being brought in. The sweetcorn bait is visible in the mouth.

Two different Carp-Goldfish hybrids caught by Mike. A fun activity but no record-breaking fish.

Notes–Sheung Pak Nai, Nim Wan Road, Pak Nai, Lau Fau Shan

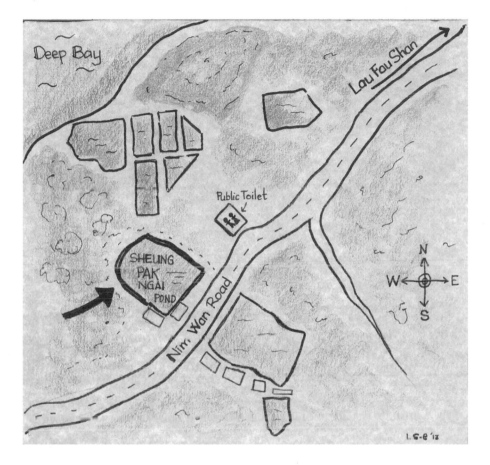

You can get there by driving or by public transport (MTR) to Tin Shui Wai via the West Rail and boarding an N.T. taxi to 'Sheung Pak Nai' (about HK$60).

You can catch a minibus for the return trip to the MTR. Octopus card is useful method of payment.

You will need 11-12ft Rod, fixed spool reel, 8-10lbs line, stick floats, ledger weights, feeders, split shot weights, landing net, live-bait box, size 12-8 hooks.

Bait: sweetcorn, paste, luncheon meat, boiled peanuts, and bread.

* (watch out for thieving cat)

Species you hope to catch are common carp, Silver Carp, Mud Carp, Big Head Carp, Catfish, Barb, Tilapia, Bream.

Ho Jie Saltwater Ponds

It was a bright sunny November day when John and I embarked on a fishing trip up to Ha Pak Nai to fish the ponds at 'Ho Jie'. This was a bit of a problem as both of us had been detained by members of our respective families at social gatherings the night before and we both had sore heads and brains that were not working at full strength. This resulted in me leaving the bait in my freezer and an uncomfortable MTR journey up to Tin Shui Wai before catching a cab to Ho Jie.

Ho Jie has two ponds and is very obvious when you arrive, as it appears as a large complex with two good sized ponds surrounded by red metal fencing.

The entrance to Ho Jie with the fishing shack in the background. Rods and bait are available however, the fishing line is old and short in length so bringing your own tackle is a good idea.

Happy local angler landing a fish.

Ho Jie Ponds are basically converted fish farming ponds with man-made sides and safety railings. Each fishing spot has chairs and table and a net on hand to help land the fish. Anglers sometimes bbq food while fishing.....and drink beer.

It looks artificial and basically it is, but the ponds are full of fish and species include Barramundi, Red Drums, Snapper, Tilapia, Amberjacks, Mullet and a resident Giant Grouper. The Chinese family running the location appeared friendly enough and charged us HK$80 each to fish the location. I checked out the toilets and found them pretty basic and traditional in design. Nevertheless, the fishing positions were clean and kitted out with tables, umbrellas and rubbish bins. There are landing nets around the place and you can get a large plastic basket to keep your catch in.

On this day, we set up in our traditional style of one rod for frozen shrimp and one rod for live shrimp. We checked the depths by plumbing and found a ledge about 4 metres out that dropped to 2.5 metres depth therefore we chose to fish the ledge with the lighter tackle (10 pound line, light float and size 10 hook). As I was not sure of the size of fish in the pond I took the precaution of adding a trace of 20 pound line two foot from the hook to a swivel so as to make sure the fish did not immediately cut the line with their gills or sharp teeth. On my second rod I employed 13 pound line and a thicker trace of 40 pound line and a larger long shank hook of about size 6. I then visited my live-bait container and found that my bubbler, which keeps the water oxygenated had got wet and broken down. The prawns were looking a bit sick so I placed them in a small plastic live bait bag and put the bag into the pond in the hope that some of them would recover. I grabbed one live prawn and hooked him through the tail and then cast out about 15 metres into the pond knowing full well that

A Red Drum being played and tangling other lines. If you want to have two rods out, its better to have a fishing buddy with you.

the prawn would take the float for a swim-about.

John had basically the same setup as me and we both fished the lighter tackle in the swims in front of us. I then catapulted large amounts of recently defrosted shrimp into the area of our floats in order to attract patrolling fish. John was the first to be into a fish with a good hard fighting Pomfret that dived and pulled everywhere. This was followed by my large prawn being taken by a nice 2-3kg Snapper, which was a pleasant surprise. We then continued to feed shrimp into our forward swim so as to attract more fish. This proved successful and during the day we caught at least another ten fish on the lighter tackle from this area.

In respect of the stronger tackle with the large prawns, we landed more Snapper and a large Tilapia. All of these fish took the prawn when it had moved to the ledge, 4 metres out. We did not hit any monster fish during our visit but saw a large amount of activity that watered our taste buds for a further attempt in the future. We did experiment with small live-baited fish instead of the prawns and these proved better than the prawns in attracting predatory Snapper. By 4:30pm we had both had enough and were running on reserve tanks so we packed up and took two of our larger fish to the shop to pay up. The staff were helpful and gutted and scaled the fish, however we were required to pay an extra HK$60 each to take these fish away. So it was not so cheap in the end.

We each only took one fish home as the cost of removal was expensive compared to the cost of fishing. In order to get back to Sai Kung we waited for the minibus to come past the fish pond and used our Octopus cards to pay the HK$9 passenger fee. This took us to Tin Shui Wai MTR where we alighted and then we made our way back to Sai Kung via the Diamond Hill interchange where we splashed out on a taxi as we were both worn out.

Amberjack. A great fighter and a very tasty fish to eat.

Notes- Ho Jie - Nim Wan Road, Pak Nai, Lau Fau Shan

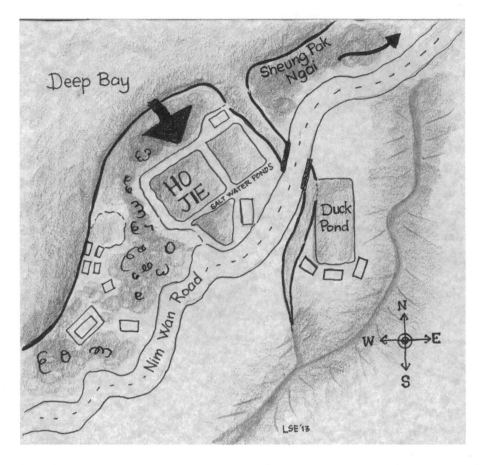

You can get there by private car; or travel to Tin Shui Wai MTR via the West Rail and board an N.T. taxi to 'Sheung Pak Nai' (HK$65).

You can catch Minibus for the return trip to MTR. Octopus card is a useful payment method for your transportation.

Tackle

You will need to bring 9ft-12ft rod, fixed spool reel, 10-15 lbs line, stick floats, ledger weights, 50lbs trace line, larger floats, spinner/plugs, landing net, live-bait box, size 12-8 hooks.

For the bait – you will need frozen krill, live green prawns, sprats deadbait, fresh squids, and lures.

Notes: Large Grouper caught here and a 15Kg Red Drum caught on lure. (Rapala Lures and surface boppers)

Hong Kong's Reservoirs

We have combined the reservoirs into one chapter as they are very difficult to handle with a limited open season. In addition, rising and falling water levels affect access to the various locations. Yet there are many, and some have interesting species to have a go at.

We suggest you practise on the ponds, and once you are happy with your fishing style, head off to the reservoirs and start to target the enormous fish that inhabit them. This is the cheapest fishing in Hong Kong, with a licence costing HK$24 and lasting three years. However, the venues are difficult as they are very large and there may not be fish resident in the area you want to fish.

To get best results it is wise for an angler to study the target water with Polaroid sunglasses and try to work out a good haunt where the fish are congregating. After that we would recommend using natural baits such as

John spinning for Large-Mouth Bass at Tai Tam.

Brides Pool , a natural river that flows into Plover Cove Reservoir. Good for a cooling dip after a hot day's fishing at the nearby ponds.

freshwater shrimp as many of the reservoir fish will not be familiar with the pastes and breads anglers normally like to place on their hooks. In addition, some reservoirs are not worth trying due to the scarcity of fish. High Island and Tai Tam Reservoirs (as opposed to Tai Tam Tuk Reservoir) are pretty devoid of fish and really not worth wasting time on. Others such as Plover Cove are absolutely loaded with fish – especially 5ft long Grass Carp, giant Big Head Carp and other large exotic species dumped by aquarium owners.

It is possible to come across South American Arowanas and American Garfish that have been illegally introduced.

Tai Tam Tuk Reservoir near Stanley is famous for Large-Mouth Bass (Gwai Far) and Snakehead (Green and Striped) and we have caught both fish by spinning along the margins (side). Early morning and evening is best for predatory fish and any angler fishing there should be lightly equipped with spinning rod and reel, landing net and a selection of spinners. That way he can roam around the area and scramble through the bushes to get at the fishing sites. The banks

Mike spinning while accompanied by daughter Jennifer who was more interested in collecting wild flowers.

Lizzie in action with her 'pink panther' outfit.

of these reservoirs are generally full of jungle foliage so going light is advisable.

Plover Cove Reservoir near Tai Po is probably the most accessible reservoir with a beautiful road running towards it which is popular with motorists. Water for the reservoir comes in from the Mainland via pipeline and from the river running from Brides Pool. There is a high algae content in the reservoir and the fish grow to enormous sizes. It is not uncommon to see Grass Carp over 50 pounds (25kg) and Big Head Carp over 100 pounds (50kg). Catching them is another matter and anglers are advised to put in some 'study time' prior to having a go. Be prepared to be disappointed as the fishing is hard and good results may not come straight away.

As I mentioned before, you will be surprised by what is swimming around in our reservoirs. We are certain that some huge carp over 50kg in weight exist in some of these locations. There are also other types of fish, both introduced and native, which can only be found in the reservoirs and are not really seen in the fish ponds as the latter are normally stocked with farmed species. Sightings of these more unusual fish become the subjects of legend as some can grow to enormous sizes and are very aggressive. We have yet to tangle with any of these monsters and plan to go after these in the future.

In summary, the reservoirs are numerous, they contain a lot of fish, and the licence is very cheap. We encourage anglers to have a go, but suggest practising at Tai Mei Tuk before heading on to the reservoirs as the conditions are very challenging.

List of Recommended Reservoirs (Accessible)

Tai Tam Tuk
Pok Fu Lam
Aberdeen Country Park Upper and Lower
Kowloon Reservoir
Shing Mun (Jubilee) Reservoir
Plover Cove Reservoir

Offshore Game Fishing around Hong Kong

Believe it or not, you can participate in offshore game fishing in the seas south of Hong Kong. There are only two drawbacks in pursuing this type of fishing, and they are 'time and money!' Firstly, you will need to cover a large area by boat to find game fish and secondly, the cost of a day out won't be less than HK$2,500. Pushing these two points aside, it is possible for an angler to pursue many types of popular gamefish that enter the waters south of Hong Kong on a seasonal basis. April to May and September to October are considered the 'hot periods' with the following species being caught by anglers:

Sailfish landed after a fierce struggle

1. Black Marlin	6. Rainbow Runners
2. Tuna (6 species)	7. Wahoo
3. Dorado	8. Trevally (Giant Trevally)
4. Chinese Mackerel	9. Barracuda
5. Sailfish	10. Cobia

All of these species can be caught by trolling (towing a lure) an area of sea up to 160km south of Hong Kong.

Kim Stuart runs such an operation out of Aberdeen called 'Tailchasers' and regularly catches many of the species mentioned above in the waters south of Hong Kong. Kim runs two types of trip and these are split between normal trolling around the areas mentioned above and south of the Lema Islands; or a visit to the Chinese oil rigs situated 65km south of Hong Kong. These structures number over 30 and attract large predatory fish who are in turn preying on the local schools of bait fish. These trips are very popular and are booked up quickly, so it is advisable that anglers keep an eye on Kim's website for updates on forthcoming trips.

So what happens in trolling? Basically, trolling means a lure is towed behind a boat at about 100-200 metres range at a speed of 7-8 knots. The lure is intended to travel about one foot (30cm) below the surface, and its reflective colours will attract predatory fish to attack it and thereby hook themselves.

Indication that a fish has taken the lure is normally demonstrated by a splash on the surface as the fish takes the lure and attempts to dive with it. The 'take' also causes the line to leave the fishing reel as the fish speeds off. The drag is set on the reel so that in most cases the hook will set itself into the mouth of the fish. However in some cases the angler will need to engage the gear on the reel and strike by raising the rod and set the hook in the fish's mouth. At this stage the fish will begin the fight and the sensation is rather like hanging onto a sports car accelerating away. Depending on the strength of the fish, anglers will need to be fitted with harnesses and a protective groin cup in which to place the rod butt. This is affectionately called the 'mangina' and you don't need any explanation of this amusing connotation.

Subsequently, like with any large fish, there will be a period where the fish will attempt to escape, and the skill and strength of the angler will be paramount in bringing the specimen to the boat. In the case of billfish such as Marlin or Sailfish, these species are brought to the boat, unhooked and released; while fish such as Tuna are generally retained as they are good to eat, unless the angler wishes them to be returned.

Offshore game fishing equipment is expensive and in particular, the large-capacity fishing reels and the line that goes on them. You cannot cheat and use cheap reels as the gears must be strong enough to withstand the workout they will receive from some of the fastest animals on the planet. So be expected to part with over HK$1,500 for a good fishing reel and another HK$500 or so for the correct line.

Of course, should you wish to follow this sport only occasionally, it is best to use the kit available with the boat operator as it will be up-to-date and the correct strength for the job in hand. In the case of Kim's boat, all kit is provided and the angler just needs to turn up. So that's Hong Kong game fishing in a nutshell. A very exclusive form of angling, which is very exciting and very expensive to pursue. Good luck!

A Dorado or Mahi-Mahi getting gaffed at the end of an exhausting fight.
Note the clear water of the South China Sea, something rarely seen
around Hong Kong's estuarine environment.

Dorado, also known as Mahi-Mahi, come into Hong Kong waters.

30Kg Wahoo

A day's catch consisting of a mix bag with Dorado, Kawa Kawa Tuna and Bluefin Tuna.

Sailfish on display with some happy anglers before being returned to fight again.

Freshly caught Yellow Fin Tuna displayed by a happy angler and a happy skipper in the background.

Pier and Island Fishing

Fishing from the piers and rocky outcrops around Hong Kong is a popular activity given that the sites are free and you can take your catch home without being charged money for doing so. The sites are as many as you can imagine, but actually finding good fishing is a skill of its own and some research and networking will be required to find the good locations where fish congregate.

Tactics are similar to freshwater fishing in that you employ either float-tackle or bottom fishing methods. In both cases, the hook length should be weaker in breaking strain to the main line to allow an angler to extract his main tackle from any snag or rocks hidden in the depths. Tide is also an important factor in sea fishing with the best fishing occurring when the tide is coming in, as fish will venture inshore and start grazing and hunting on the newly flooded areas.

Consequently, one should pay attention to the tide tables published by the Hong Kong Observatory. The seasons also affect the fishing with the best fishing to be had between September and December when fish come into Hong Kong waters. Hong Kong suffers from over-fishing by trawlers and the Government is now doing something about it by buying up the trawler fleet. This is good news; however, it is still wise to keep any information on good sites quiet as local net fishermen may get wind of the location and come and empty it out.

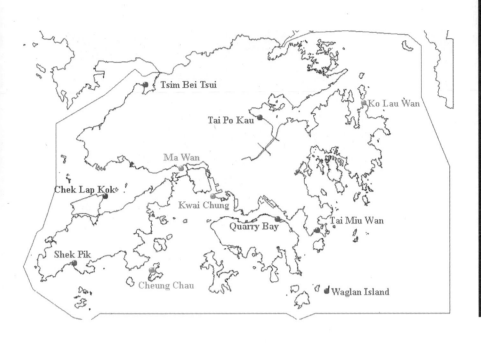

Tap Mun Island; otherwise known as Grass Island is popular with fishermen, campers and day trippers. It has a famous seafood restaurant located in the main village which serves good helpings of popular dishes such as deep fried squid, steamed prawns and clams.

Popular fishing channel ('South Channel') between Tap Mun and Ko Lau Wan Tsui

John pictured sitting on Tap Mun Pier keeping an eye out for incoming ferries and providing photo opportunities for visiting tourists.

Pier Fishing

Pier fishing is a popular pastime in Hong Kong. The structures give anglers the chance to fish over deep water where the fish are more likely to be, and the structures in return attract fish to loiter around them. Piers always have lighting, and lights at night attract fry or small fish. Anglers like to call these fish 'Baitfish'. Consequently the baitfish are followed in by predatory fish such as Snapper, Bass and Squid who will charge into the shoals grabbing the plentiful supply of small fish. In warm weather, and at high tide, anglers often catch squid off the piers around Sai Kung for the very same reasons I have mentioned before.

The same phenomenon applies in the winter when the sea temperature drops below 17 degrees. Bass will come in from the cold deep water to hunt, and they like to visit the piers and anchorages where security and mooring lights attract fry. They are one of the sought-after targets of sea anglers, who will turn out and fish in any conditions once word of their arrival in Hong Kong waters spreads. Popular venues are the Central Piers, Kowloon City Pier, and any other pier or structure where lighting attracts baitfish.

Pier fishing methods are similar and cruder versions of freshwater methods. An ideal rod is about 10-12 ft long (3.5-4 metres) fitted with a standard fishing reel with 12-15 pound (5-7 kg) line. There are three main methods which an angler can employ and these will account for most situations.

Tso Wo Hang old Police pier. A very popular angling site with local anglers

Method One – Straight Ledger

Run a 2-ounce weight up the main line. Follow with a bead and then tie the main line to the swivel thereby preventing the ledger from leaving the main line. Add a 1-2 ft hook length or trace to the other end of the swivel and tie a hook size 10-4. This trace should be weaker than the main line so you can break free if entangled or hooked onto any snag. Bites are indicated by the rod tip bending or by the feeling in your finger if you hold the line.

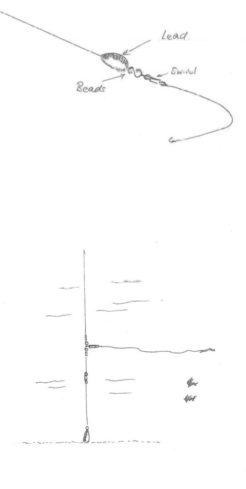

Method Two – Paternoster

Run a 'float stop' (you can buy these) up the main line. Follow with a bead and then a free-running swivel followed by a bead and another float stop and then secure the end of the line onto a swivel. Attach a 2-3 ft trace from the free running swivel of similar strength to the main line and attach a hook size 8-2. Then attach a weaker length of line from the swivel attached to the main line of about one metre in length to a 2-oz weight. This will allow the weight to break free in the event of lead being caught in a snag. The float stops allow the trace to be fished at any depth from one to three metres off the bottom and it will simply fly in the current. In similar manner to the method above, bites will be indicated by the rod tip bending or by the line pulling against your finger or reel drag.

Method Three – Sliding Float

Floats are always easy to watch. Simply find a large float and run the line through its bottom ring. Take the main line down to a swivel and then add a trace of thicker line to a hook. The trace should be about 0.4m long. Add some weights to the main line to cock the float and provide casting weight. In order to stop the line simply passing through the float ring you tie a piece of rubber band onto the main line above the float and then slide this band to the right depth you wish to fish at.

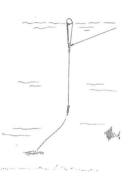

When you cast, it is easy for the band to pass through the rod rings and for it to cock the float into position at the prescribed depth. Bites are indicated by the float being pulled underwater. One of the tricks of this method is to make sure the rubber band is small enough to pass through the rings of the rod, otherwise the tackle will be impossible to use at the right depth.

Secondly, when you are night fishing, it is possible to purchase floats with fittings that allow luminous strips to be attached so that you can see the float at night. This is useful for Bass fishing as they normally come in at night during the winter. This method is also applicable to rock fishing.

Local Sai Kung angler Jeff, with a 1Kg Red Drum caught off the sea wall with ledgered squid during high tide at night. This fish was caught in December time and was a surprise as we had not expected to catch anything significant that evening.

Island Fishing

Island fishing is more of a day trip, and packing swimming trunks is a very good idea. Around Sai Kung there are many islands where you can spend the day – exploring, barbecuing and, more importantly, fishing. In fact, during those sensitive times when the family may not be as interested in fishing as you are, you can suggest an island trip and incorporate an hour or two of fishing while everyone else is swimming or sunbathing. Fishing on islands basically involves a combination of beach, rock and pier fishing with the same methods mentioned previously. The key to all of this is to know the ferry operators and their timings. Many of the islands around Sai Kung town can be reached by purchasing a return ticket for just HK$38 and a sampan will drop you off and pick you up at the end of the day. It is important that you get the mobile phone number of the sampan operator and let them know when you wish to be picked up.

Heavily barnacled Government pier in Sai Kung

Selection of fish landed while rock fishing

Fishing off rocks has its risks and care should be taken to make sure you have an escape route if the weather gets worse or the tide rises. Strong footwear is a definite requirement, and so is adequate clothing to protect you against the sun. If you visit the local tackle shops you can find fishing waistcoats that have been combined into life vests and walking boots with thick soles that will grip wet rocks. Should you have the funds, there is no harm in investing in any of these items to improve your safety.

When fishing off islands, I use a ledger with the weight located at the bottom of the line, 'paternoster' fashion. That way, crabs cannot sneak up, drag your bait off into a rocky hole and snag your line. I like to use my telescopic rod as it is both portable and convenient when moving on and off boats and across rocky coastlines. Line should be 10 pounds upwards and a good supply of hooks and weights is important. Squid and worms have proven to be the most convenient baits and during those times when I have not had any prepared baits I will scrape shellfish off the rocks and stick the innards onto the hook.

Given that islands around Hong Kong are generally isolated it is a good idea to take a freezer bag or box in order to store drinks and preserve any fish caught. You can discover the islands and ferry times from the standard local travel books or visit the Hong Kong Ferries website for timings to outlying islands. Island fishing is a bit of an adventure and a nice way to spend a day in Hong Kong.

A freshly caught Pipe fish taken by Mike at Tap Mun Pier on squid.
It was quickly returned as we could see there was not much to eat on this species.

*Al fresco cooking is always good fun whilst fishing off the islands of Hong Kong.
I know this is a book about fishing however the lamb cutlets did taste very good!*

The view of Lau Fau Shan from Yau Ley Restaurant at High Island Reservoir

FISHING TIPS *and* GENERAL ADVICE

The Fishing Seasons

For ease of explanation, I have divided Hong Kong's weather patterns into four seasons. The timing of these seasons may alter by one to two months depending on the weather patterns in the South China Sea and the Pacific. The seasons affect the fishing and sometimes you will not achieve much as you have chosen the wrong time to go. So appreciating the seasonal variations is important. Temperature change, tidal flow and bright sunlight all affect fish in just the same way as a human being decides what level of outdoor activity they should follow.

Sai Kung coastline near Tai Long Wan during a cool winter's evening.

Winter

Cold and windy with temperatures down to 5 degrees centigrade. Fishing is not so good in both freshwater and saltwater environments. In winter, freshwater fish will generally feed between sunrise and sunset, about 10am-4pm. The fish will shoal and stay in fixed locations and be attracted to warm-water outlets such as nullahs. When it is cold, both fish and anglers do not feel like taking part in the sport; apart from Sea Bass, who are at home in cold temperatures and come into the coastal waters.

Spring

Spring brings warm and humid air with temperatures rising to 15-22 degrees centigrade. Fish activity increases rapidly, however monsoon rain in May and June will temporarily lower the water temperature and put off freshwater fish for a while until the sun warms the water again. Therefore, fishing in rainstorms is not advisable, and fishing rods are good at attracting lightning so anglers should seek cover if a thunderstorm arrives. Fishing is good between dawn and about 1pm.

Bride's Pool with Mike's daughter and friend enjoying themselves.

Summer

Extremely hot weather with temperatures up to 33 degrees centigrade is prevalent throughout the summer months of July to September. Fishing is uncomfortable for both the angler and for the freshwater fish, especially when the sun is at its highest point, as the brightness hurts their vision. Fish normally feed at dawn or dusk or within shaded areas. Anglers get baked, and if without appropriate clothing or shelter, will come to harm. Passing typhoons can adversely affect fishing activity and any wind warning above the Typhoon 3 signal should be avoided. However, in summer it is possible to do well, especially during early morning fishing sessions in lakes or out at sea when the squid come into coastal waters.

A view of the spectacular volcanic rock formations found around the Nine Pin Islands off Sai Kung.

Autumn

Autumn is the best time of year for fishing – the weather is cooler and there is less rain. Fishing is good both at sea, when species move into shallow water to breed, and inland at freshwater locations as the weather is pleasurable and bearable. This is the best time of year for barbecues on the beach, picnics by the lakes, and good swimming. Fishing is always fun during the autumn months up until about mid-December when the temperature starts to drop.

Picturesque Sai Kung coastline.

The coastline near Tai O on Lantau during an Autumn evening. Just as the sun is going down.

Fishing Knots

There are many different types of knot, but the average angler can get by after learning four basic knots, and these are reproduced for you below.

The Half Blood (for securing hooks to line)

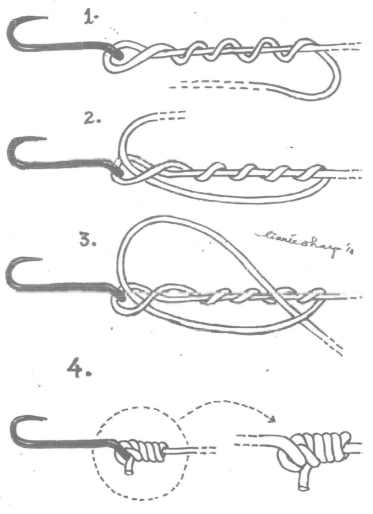

1. Thread the line through the eye and twist 5-6 times around the mainline.

2. Thread the line through the bottom loop.

3. Thread line through the main loop in order to lock the line.

4. Finished knot should have a pile of coils over the eye.

This knot is normally about 80% secure, however, should you be chasing sizeable fish such as catfish or large carp or sea fish, then the other knots should be considered.

To make the knot stronger we sometimes tuck the line back through as demonstrated of put the mainline through the hook eye twice before starting the knot.

The Palomar Knot (for securing hooks to line)

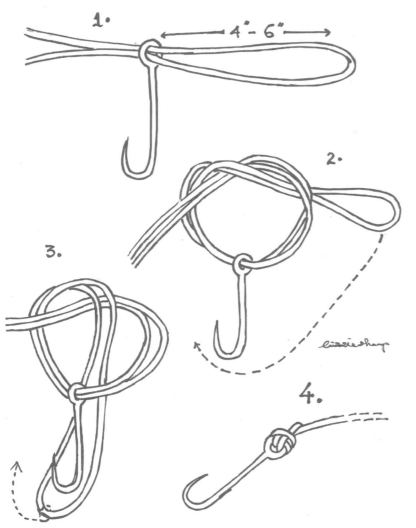

1. ←— 4"– 6" —→

Push a loop of line through the eye of the hook.

2.

Form a simple loop with a tuck.

3.

4.

Pull the loop at the end over the complete Hook and pull tight.

This knot is very good for saltwater lines as it is easy to manipulate the thick lines to form an effective knot. This knot is used very safe and the chance of undoing or breakage is slim.

You will probably need to photocopy this image and take it with you if you are unfamiliar.

The Blood Knot (for joining two lines)

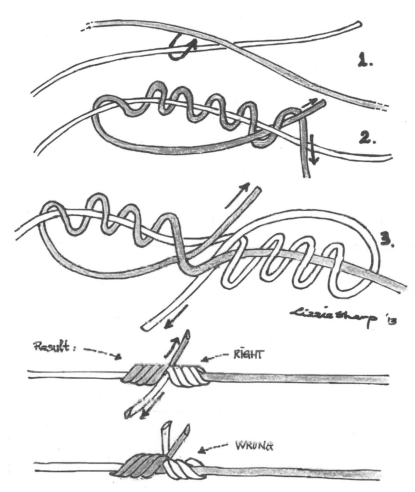

1. Place one line over the other.

2. Twist the lines together and then thread the ends through the centre gap from opposing directions.

3.

Result:

RIGHT

WRONG

Carefully pull tight and the finished knot should look like the top example

The Blood Knot is used for joining two lines together. It is about 70% safe with lines of similar diameter. It is impractical for putting a thick 25 pound line to 10 pound line and other options should be looked at. It is a fiddly knot and needs a bit of practice.

The knot is useful for making tapered traces for fly fishing where the thick fly line is attached to monofilament line that starts at 20 pound and tapers through 15, 12, 8 and down to 5 pound line. The tapering allows for better flight and presentation of the fly.

The Loop (for attaching traces and tackle items)

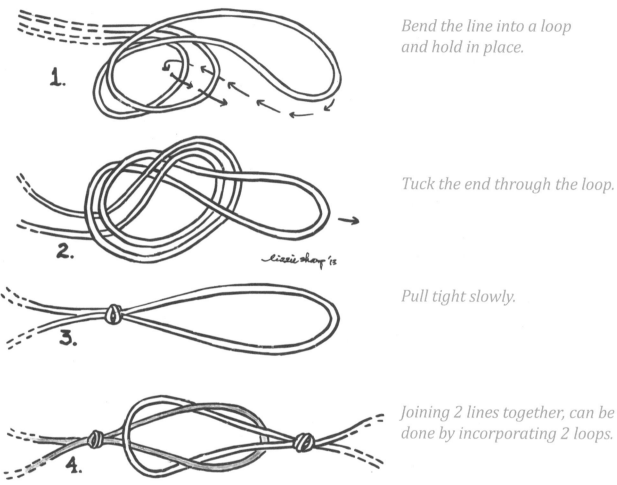

1.

Bend the line into a loop and hold in place.

2.

Tuck the end through the loop.

3.

Pull tight slowly.

4.

Joining 2 lines together, can be done by incorporating 2 loops.

The above loop can be made stronger by turning it into a 'figure-of-eight' knot however, the knot that we have shown is good enough to secure tackle and especially good when using braid fishing line.

When we prepare traces, they are normally finished off with this knot so that during the on-site tackle preparation, the loop makes the setting up very simple. The knot is also good for joining two lines of different sizes (thickness) or attaching traces or even conducting emergency repairs.

Tackle Tips

Freshwater Float Fishing

Float fishing in Hong Kong is predominantly stillwater as there are few freshwater rivers worthy of attention. Therefore, presentation of bait by float must follow three rules:

- The hookbait must fall naturally to the bottom of the swim, and;

- The hookbait should not move once it has touched the bottom or targeted depth and;

- The depth of the water should be checked to make sure the hook bait touches the bottom.

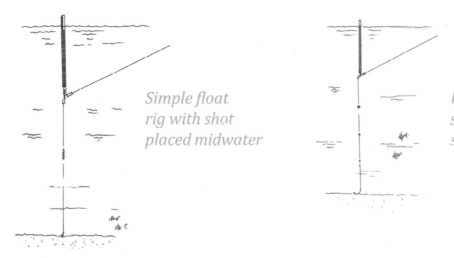

Simple float rig with shot placed midwater

Float rig with spaced shot-pattern : Largest shot nearest the float.

Given that float fishing is not easy, the following guide has been prepared to assist the freshwater fisherman master this aspect of the sport.

Firstly, attach all floats at the bottom by using either lead shot or float stops. Then, sink the line between the float and the rod by pushing the tip of the rod underwater and winding the float onto the required position. This will stop the wind blowing the float off position. Apply a little bit of detergent to the first 3 metres of line so that it will immediately sink through the surface film. The position of the

shot will affect the performance of the float. This means you can either place the shot nearer the hook and lay the weight of the shot on the bottom or you can move the shot up the line and space it out to allow the bait to drift into position.

Also, should you wish to cast a considerable distance (say over 10 metres) then it's best if you move the shot up the line so that they are positioned directly under the float. This makes for a more dynamic package that will fly through the air better when cast and land in the water without any tangles occurring.

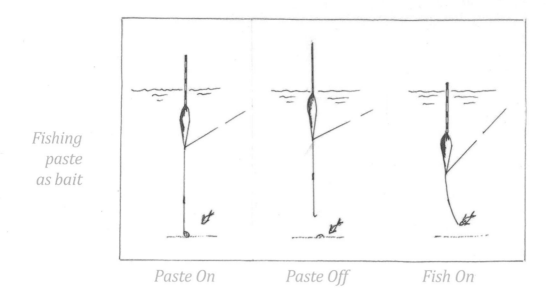

Paste On *Paste Off* *Fish On*

The practice of 'Plumbing' means carrying out an essential skill to find out the depth of the water and help decide what level (bottom / midwater or surface) you wish to fish. Attach the plummet (large weight) to the hook and drop the float rig into the swim. If the float disappears under water then the distance between the float and hook is too short. Pull it out and adjust the float and re-try. Ideally you should see the first 2cm of the float with the hook lying on the bottom.

When a float sits in the water, about 10mm-15mm of the top should be visible on the surface. This cuts down on the resistance felt by the fish when it pulls on the hook bait. In the case of the local 'needle floats', these are

deigned to expose the striped section so that you can assess confidently when a carp has decided to take the bait or when the paste has dropped off the hook. The following diagrams demonstrate this;

It is also advisable to tie a trace using fluorocarbon line; which is more transparent and less reflective. It should also be slightly weaker breaking strain between the hook and the mainline so that the fish has less chance of seeing it and if you get snagged, you will have less chance of losing all of the terminal tackle. Carp have a habit of sucking and blowing so it is likely that you will see your float moving around a bit before a carp decides to take the bait and swim off. Making a judgment on when to strike the hook home takes practice and is part of the fun of fishing. A rough guide is to wait until the float dips in a definite movement.

Chinese Needle Floats with a double hook length.

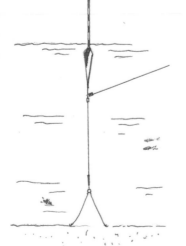

Chinese Needle Floats

58

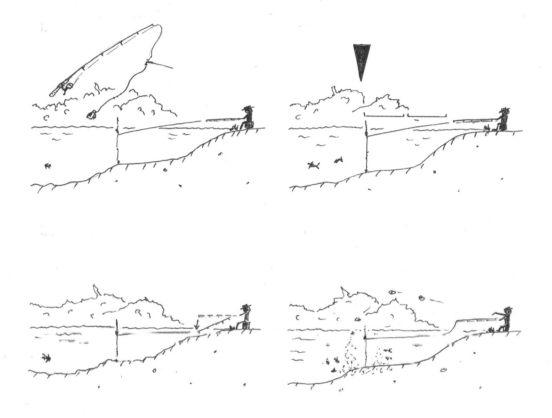

Step 1

Angler surveys his fishing area by using a plummet weight attached to his hook. He moves his float up and down the line depending on the depth so that the hook rests on the bottom and the float sits at the correct level.

Step 2

Angler memorises the selected fishing spot by rod lengths and reference points. He should cast into the same area.

Step 3

Angler sinks the line by pushing rod tip underwater. He can also add some detergent to the line to make it sink. That way the wind does not drag the float off target.

Step 4

The angler should focus on casting to the same spot. He should then throw his ground-bait into the same location so that his hook bait and ground bait are together. Fish will arrive to investigate the ground-bait and hopefully take the hook bait.

Ledgering

Ledgering is the most common form of bottom fishing. The tackle is simple and you place a baited hook attached to a weight in an area where you think fish are and wait for the rod tip to move, or you feel a bite by keeping the line around your finger.

Unfortunately it is a bit more complicated and in this section I shall describe three types of bottom fishing and the tackle required.

Rods and Reels

Rods should be 8 ft plus and of a more rigid design than those normally used for float fishing. A 10-11 ft spinning rod can be used if no UK specialist rod is available. The ideal reel is a bait-runner which will allow the line to leave the reel when a fish takes the bait in a controlled manner.

By turning the handle and engaging the drag on the reel an angler can make contact with the line and strike the hook into place. If a bait-runner reel is not available then an angler can loosen the spool on the reel so that line runs off the reel when a fish takes the bait. To strike, the angler merely grabs the spool, lifts the rod to set the hook and then tightens the front drag on the spool.

Bait Runner Fishing Reel
Note : the extra lever at the end of
the reel used to engage the line release.

Terminal Tackle

Generally, when ledgering, the takes or bites involve the fish suddenly becoming aware of being hooked and turning and making a run for an underwater obstacle such as a weed bed or jetty etc. In addition, we are chasing large fish who can generate a large amount of pull once engaged on the tackle. This entails the use of fishing line which is not less than 10 pound breaking strain.

At the working end or where the terminal tackle is, I will explain three methods with which you can set up effective ledgering techniques to catch carp and catfish and keep them on the line!

Basic Ledger

This is the simplest set-up and you will find this method used by both fresh and salt water anglers.

Thread the main line through a lead weight and a bead and tie it to a swivel. Attach a hook length of approximately 16cm length to the swivel and tie on a Size 10 hook. The hook length needs to be slightly weaker than the mainline so that if the tackle is snagged, the line can be broken without losing the rest of the tackle. Bites are indicated by the line being pulled off the reel if a Bait Runner is used or if some visible indicator like a piece of silver foil is used.

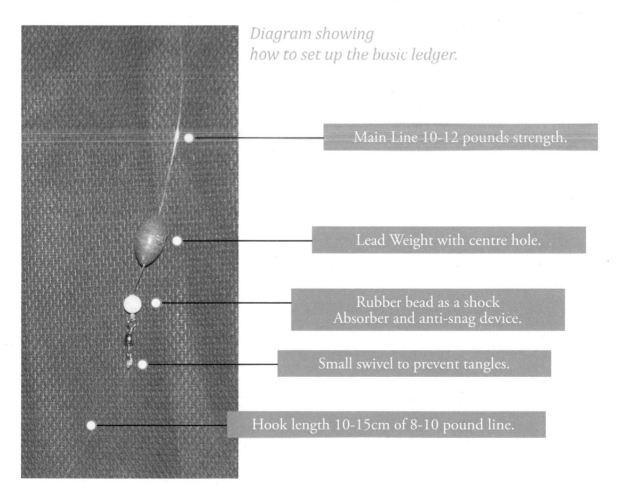

Diagram showing how to set up the basic ledger.

Main Line 10-12 pounds strength.

Lead Weight with centre hole.

Rubber bead as a shock Absorber and anti-snag device.

Small swivel to prevent tangles.

Hook length 10-15cm of 8-10 pound line.

Feeder Fishing

A feeder is a small cage into which you squeeze groundbait and hook bait. The feeder is used instead of the lead weight as it has a lead strip inserted inside it. The tackle set up is the same as the basic ledger however the style of fishing is slightly different. Basically the feeder allows an angler to deliver bait to the area where he is fishing so during the first hour of fishing he should cast to his fishing point frequently in order that a carpet of bait is released over the lake bottom.

Each time he has cast, he should tighten up the line so that a small bend exists in the rod. When a fish takes, the rod will either spring straight as line goes slack or curve round further, in both cases the angler should strike. The rod should always be placed at angle or right angle to the line so that the bend is very visible to the angler.

Method Feeder – A method feeder is similar to a normal cage feeder in that it is designed to deliver more bait to the area being fished so that the fish will come and feed around the hook. The method feeder however, is bigger and a large ball of ground bait can be attached to it so that a lot of bait will surround the hook and attract the fish. Bites are indicated by employing a bait runner reel so that when the line runs out the angler should strike into the fish. In respect of the method feeder, a strong rod should be used as the bait can weigh quite a bit and stress the rod when casting.

Open-ended feeders with and without bait. (Two beads have been placed between the feeder and swivel to act as shock absorbers)

One type of flat-bottomed method feeder, with and without bait. Note the short hook length.

Carp Hair Rig

In the above rigs I have not mentioned anything special about the hook bait and basically, an angler simply fills the hook with his bait to make it attractive and hope that the fish does not detect the presence of the metal hook. In order to make the hookbait more deceptive anglers sometimes secure an extra length of monofilament line or braid onto the hook in order to further deceive the fish.

The extra bit of line is called the 'hair rig' and it places the bait off the hook so that the fish will not detect the metal hook when it samples the bait. A baiting needle is a must in order to aid the angler place bait onto the rig. The next series of photos and diagrams show the method to set up a hair rig.

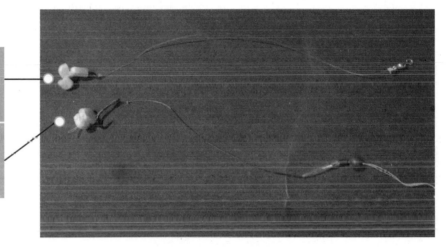

Standard hook-length with bait placed on hook to hide the point.

Hair rig showing the bait threaded onto a line extended from the hook.

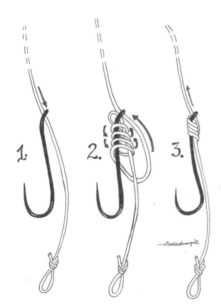

How to tie a Carp Hair Rig

- Pass a length of monofilament line or braid, through the eye of the hook with a small loop tied at the end.

- Place the length of line with the loop against the hook and bring the end without the loop and wind down the hook towards the bend before tucking it back through the hook eye.

- Slowly pull tight.

Bait

This chapter is split into two as there are marked differences between freshwater and saltwater baits. I will limit the potential Hong Kong angler to those baits we know will work.

There are obvious differences between the two categories and the baits listed here are the easiest to obtain.

fresh water bait

Freshwater Baits

Sweetcorn

Sweetcorn is both brightly coloured and strong enough to stay on the hook while an angler is casting a bait, especially over long distances. It can also be flavoured and coloured to increase attractiveness. When you open the sweetcorn packet, empty out the brine (liquid) and pour the sweetcorn pieces into a bowl of water in order to remove the saltiness. You can then use the kernels as they are, or add cake colouring if you want to change the corn's colour. While fishing, you should ensure that the point of hook is visible to allow for easy hooking of fish when they bite.

Bread

This bait is not as good in Hong Kong as it is in the UK and Europe but it can certainly prove useful as a surface bait if it is dried out. Remember to thread the hook and line through the crust before casting the crust out to the water surface, as the fish will try and break it down and cause the hook to fall away. Mullet that like to hang around harbour environments also like bread as they are accustomed to hunting for scrap food entering the water.

These baits have mixed results in Hong Kong but should not be ignored. Worms or 'Night Crawlers' can be found under leaves near bushes and trees in damp areas if they haven't already been taken by wild boar! They are very active wrigglers and after being placed on a hook their movement will attract fish. They should be hooked at least twice as fish have an annoying habit of biting off the tails without taking the whole bait, resulting in missed bites. Grubs are just big maggots and can be purchased from pet shops which sell reptiles. Just hook them from the fat end and let them wriggle about. Wash your hands after handling grubs as they have been bred on rotting meat and will be carrying a lot of germs.

Live Bait

The term 'live bait' refers to small fish such as young Tilapia, which you attach to the line by hooking them through the tail fin. Large predatory fish such as Catfish, Snakehead and Predatory Carp will attack the fish and become hooked. An angler will either rely on small fish he has hooked out on bait or simply purchase a packet of live silver fish from a Mong Kok aquarium where they are sold to keepers for the larger types of aquarium fish

Live bait that can be used for Snakehead and other predators.

Paste

Paste is a combination of powdered food mixed together with a binder, the latter being a sticky substance that causes the mixture to form a tight ball that will stay on the hook. There are numerous types and anglers like to add their own flavourings to make the mixture more attractive. Simply put, you should purchase a couple of bags of paste from a tackle shop and mix them equally with a binding agent into a doughy ball from which you can break off smaller balls of bait. You then squeeze these around the hook to totally conceal it. Paste is a very popular bait with Chinese fishermen using whips and they will often add their own special additives.

Freshwater Shrimps

Freshwater shrimp can be seen in all Hong Kong freshwater locations and in addition you might spot crab as well. The shrimp often come to an angler's swim when he is dropping bits of bait into the water to clean up the scraps and we often scoop them up with a fine net and use them for bait.

Carp and Catfish find shrimp irresistible and they are a 'killer bait' if you can get some. Given that they are a natural bait they are very good for those locations where man-made bait, such as paste, has not been introduced. Shrimps should be hooked through the last segment of the tail in order that they swim around and look alive.

salt water bait

Squid

Squid are easy to find in both wet markets and modern supermarkets. They are cheap, effective bait and are taken by most sea fish. The great thing with squid is that it stays on the hook and you can increase the size from tiny bits to large 30cm baits of whole squid for large fish such as Grouper. There is no set way to hook squid apart from making sure it is properly secured by perhaps threading the hook twice through the flesh or using two hooks.

Fish

Pieces of chopped fish are also respected as a bait. In fact, sea fish will eat almost anything due to the considerable competition in the marine environment for available food. Whole fish such as Sardines are used for large predatory fish such as Marlin, Swordfish, Grouper and so on, while small strips are good for estuarine or reef fish. In the case of whole fish bait, it is important that an angler secures the bait with two hooks so that the fish, which is dead, is presented in a realistic manner and the strike of the predator will not just destroy the bait. In most cases the bait should be attached so that the tail is up the line and the head is facing the hook. That way the fish will cast easier and most predators eat fish head first.

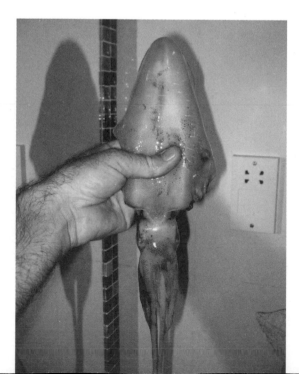

Artificial Baits: Plugs, Jigging Lures, Poppers and Plastic Fish Spinners

Ragworm

Ragworm is a good bait for estuarine fish such as Bream, Mudjacks, Mullet etc. and can be purchased live from tackle shops. They are well known because they have two nasty pincers that come out of the head and will bite the fingers of any unwary angler. In order to defeat this hazard, you can use a pair of scissors to chop the head off; or take your hook, prod the head so that they stick out their pincers, and push the hook into its mouth and thread them on. They are pretty ugly and if you want to see their nightmarish cousin then look up the 'bobbitt worm' – there you can find a very unpleasant species named after Wayne Bobbitt who lost his manhood to his angry wife. You can read up on the rest.

Prawns

These are a very good bait if they can be kept alive. When you visit the market you should buy about half a catty and try to make sure you get them from a stallholder who has a basket with them still alive and kicking. You will also need to buy a bait box with a bubbler to keep them active, and get a small bait bag which you can drop into the swim with your prawns inside so that they stay alive. As with freshwater shrimps, you should hook them in the last segment of the tail so that they can swim around. If you don't use them all up then you can take them home and freeze them and fry them up at a later date.

Groundbait

Groundbait means bait that you throw into the area where you are going to fish to attract your target species to your location or 'swim'. In freshwater, it is normally a mixture of powder, fish meal and cereals on top of which you scatter samples of the hookbait. During the fishing session you should throw in groundbait continuously, say every 15 minutes, in order to keep fish interested in your swim. This is called 'constant feed' and is a very important aid to good fishing as anglers have a habit of throwing groundbait all at once and wondering why their fishing dies out halfway through the day. Choice of material is up to the angler. Personally I like to use porridge oats mixed with purchased bags of groundbait along with some smelly additives, cake mix, etc.

Sweetcorn added to a mix of oatmeal and purchased groundbait

In the saltwater environment, groundbait is referred to as 'burley' and anglers generally use chopped fish innards and other scraps and blood from the market. The burley is placed in a net and hung in the water so that the particles of flesh, blood and oil trickle out and form a trail that fish will follow. It's hoped that fish will swim up the trail to the location where the angler is fishing. Krill (pictured right) can also be used as 'burley'.

Krill – small frozen shrimp

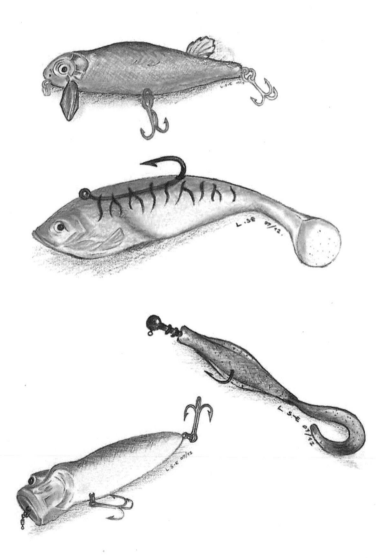

Fly-Fishing in Hong Kong

The sport of fly-fishing is a huge subject and carries its own culture and rules. It is closer to hunting than mainstream course or bait-fishing as you are normally fishing for a fish that you can see or into an area where you are pretty certain fish will be lying. Skills such as observation and stalking are called for, plus a great deal of patience. In Hong Kong, the water is generally coloured apart from our mountain streams and the lakes and ponds are full of algae and 'run-off' which is another term for silt. Still, it is possible to pursue this sport in Hong Kong with the right choice of imitation fly or other aquatic creature.

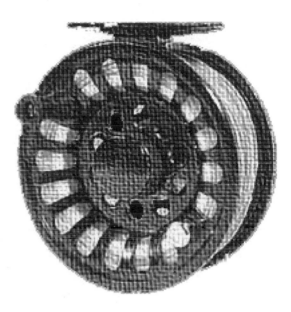

Fly-fishing by definition is the art of presenting an imitation fly to a fish in such a manner that the fish will take it in the belief that it is a genuine one. In order to achieve this task, anglers will employ a whippy style rod, a centre pin reel and a thick tapered line ('fly line') which can generate its own casting weight by moving it backwards and forwards in the air. The end of the thick casting line will be a trace of monofilament line to which the fly or lure will be attached. The traces are normally 3-4 metres in length and are of various strengths depending on the type of fish being targeted.

Casting a fly line is a skill on its own and before any beginner attempts to visit a water, he or she should visit an open area such as a sports ground and practise the cast. I should point out that even if practising, a trace should be fitted to the fly line to achieve the right motion. You can even attach a piece of bright wool at the end to represent the fly to ensure that you are allowing the 'fishing bit' to land in a realistic manner. The fly or lure is a hook onto which feathers, wool and other material are attached in such a manner as to represent a living insect or fish once in the water. These are artistic creations themselves and anglers like to collect numerous patterns. Some anglers will tie their own flies and this is viewed as an important skill connected to the sport.

There are two types of fly fishing: dry- and wet-fly fishing. In dry-fly fishing the angler aims to imitate flies dropping onto the surface film of the water. If the fish is deceived, it will rise and take the fly from the surface and you can strike and hook the fish. Wet-fly fishing is when the angler presents the fly or lure either below the surface film, to represent a hatching nymph, or deeper to represent a small fish or other crustacean.

In Hong Kong, wet-fly fishing is probably the most effective method and anglers should try and imitate nymphs and small fry just below the surface. Grass Carp, Common Carp, Snakehead and Tilapia will all take a fly in freshwater and in the case of saltwater, you can try to tempt Red Drum and Mangrove Jacks with 'fish-like' lures. However, in respect of the saltwater species, having a large-capacity reel with several hundred metres of line is necessary as the fish will run and take a lot of line if hooked.

Tenkara fishing

Tenkara is a Japanese form of dry-fly fishing where an angler uses a very light pole or whip onto which is attached a length of elastic and thin monofilament line. The angler gently lowers his imitation fly onto the surface of the water above the fish and waits for the fish to rise and snatch his fly. This form of fishing is generally aimed at those species of fish inhabiting streams, as casting for them is very difficult. In addition, if a fish decides to fight hard, an angler can only control it by raising and lowering the pole as he cannot give line because the tackle is fixed. Anyone interested in this form of fishing can visit web sites dedicated to it and these contain videos of anglers landing much larger fish using up-scaled equipment of stronger breaking strain.

Bass Flies which can be used in the marine environment
as they imitate small fish.

TARGETING SPECIES

This section offers specialised tips *from John on targeting several key species which are common in both fresh and saltwater environments in Hong Kong and are fun to catch.*

Surface Fishing for Grass Carp

Grass Carp or 'Lei Yue' are a common Chinese Carp and are farmed heavily both in Mainland China and the New Territories. Therefore, they often turn up in the various day-ticket waters around Hong Kong and can be seen swimming around in the fish section of the wet markets and main supermarkets. One fun way of catching them is to fish a float with all of the weight (lead shot) secured underneath the float. The line should be about one third of the depth and no shot should be placed near the hook. This will allow the bait to gently drop through the water when it is cast into the swim. Grass Carp like to patrol lakes and rivers within the first three feet of water and the shape of their heads seem to be similar to Saltwater Mullet who also like to look up to see what food is landing near the surface. You can often see bow waves caused by Grass Carp as they swim below the surface coupled with the occasional splash as they throw themselves out of the water or dive deep.

Sweetcorn is an ideal bait for this method and in order to deceive the carp into thinking that the hook bait falling through the water is the same as other food entering the water, the angler should throw in 4-6 particles at a time into the fishing area or swim. The hook should be small either a 12 or 14 and the float should be cast out over and past the baited area and then slowly brought into the swim by gently winding-in so that the corn raises in the water and then drops again as if it is falling from the surface. 3-4 raises will be enough to cross the swim and then the process is repeated with more loose-fed particles being added to keep the fish interested. Bites are generally savage as the fish are being extra-competitive to get to the surface food, so the line should be kept straight and fairly tight.

John with a good Grass Carp at Tai Mei Tuk

Other species such as Common Carp and Big Head Carp will go for this method, especially in warm weather when they become more active and enter shallower depths. The key to this method is a constant feed of sweetcorn grains entering the water and after 20-30 minutes, fish will start to patrol and feed in your swim.

Paste or bread is also effective and should be presented in a similar way. Take care when striking the hook home as the short length of line below the float presents less of a resistance and the float and tackle can fly past you at great speed if there is nothing on the end.

Hong Kong visitor Larry with another Grass Carp safely landed using sweetcorn placed upon a size 10 hook and attached to a coil (hair curler) style method feeder. The ground bait was made up of a combination of oatmeal, purchased groundbait and commercial fish feed.

Fishing for Moray Eels

Moray eels may not be every angler's favourite species but in Hong Kong they are here in abundance and relatively easy to catch, even when all other species refuse to eat. Most piers and jetties will hold a few resident eels, as will rocky outcrops where there is a reasonable depth and enough food around. If they are living near shallow water, then you should only attempt to fish for them at night as they are too cautious of moving about in daylight. If however they are in deep water then they can be fished for in both day and night.

If you go and see them in the aquarium, you will notice that the eels like to conceal part of their long body in holes or crevasses and they generally like to ambush their prey. Then suddenly, when there is food about, they launch out of their lair and viciously attack their prey in a matter of seconds. Applying this to the angling world, we need to present bait very near the sides of a pier or wall so that they see or smell it and come out and grab it. Best baits for Moray Eels are fish sections (fillets), squid or prawns. If you have enough bait then scatter some samples a bit away from the pier or rocks to draw the eels out and then present a similar sized hook-bait in the area.

When an eel bites at your bait the take will be quite light, similar to that of a crab playing with the bait. Following this, he will try and reverse back into his lair to consume his prize in peace. Any angler believing that a moray eel is on the end should then strike and pull hard

to remove the threat of the eel wrapping itself around a pillar or entering a hole.

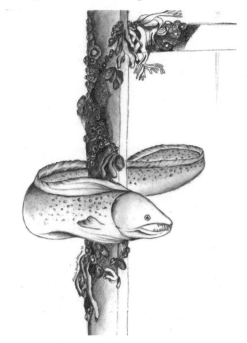

Once the latter happens it is very difficult to extract them. So any strikes should be followed up with a large tug to lift the eel away from any obstacles. One of the key points when fishing for this type of fish is to use a simple ledger and have a short trace, meaning the line between the weight and the hook. This can be 8-10 cm and be of a strong line or wire so that they cannot bite through it. The short trace prevents the eel from taking the bait into its lair and tangling it before the angler has realised he has a bite. The main line should be 30-40 pound breaking strain so that the eel can be hauled way from any obstacles.

If the eel is landed onto the pier it will immediately try and wrap itself up in coils and tangle the line and weight up. It also has sharp teeth which will be used against the angler, given the chance. So have an old towel at hand or some thick gardening gloves and grip the eel with these before using a pair of long pliers to remove the hook.

Red Drum

Red Drums, otherwise known as 'Reds', are a non-native species that have escaped from fish farms and taken up residence around Hong Kong. They can be caught in sizes up to 12-14kgs in fish ponds however, around the wild Sai Kung coastline they normally reach 2-3 kgs. They are easy to recognise, with a large black spot on their tail and a cod-like head. They like to swim around mangroves where they prey on small fry and prefer shallow water, which they enter when the light is going. By keeping still, and looking through the surface glare of the water I have spotted them sometimes swimming around and stalked them with a piece of squid on a light ledger.

Although they are quite common around our shoreline I would recommend watching the tides and focusing your efforts onto the high tide, especially if it is at night. This will encourage the Reds to swim inshore and along harbour walls and under piers.

A size 6 hook with either a live prawn or a piece of squid float fished or ledgered will catch fish. The bites are very positive and in the case of live prawn, you should allow the fish a few seconds to take the whole prawn into its mouth before striking and setting the hook home. A good sized 'Red' will put up a substantial fight and in Florida they are regarded as a sporting fish similar to the Australian Barramundi. You would not want to use fishing line less than 10 pounds breaking strain and while playing fish, an angler should keep his eye out for any underwater obstacles.

You can catch this species on spinners, plugs or wet flies as they are aggressive feeders and when hunting they will often attack any of these, providing anglers with heart-stopping moments when they pounce on the passing lure. Best time is a high tide over rocky bottom when light is fading. They will hunt at this time and become easier to catch.

Alex with a Red Drum caught at Luk Keng.

77

Mullet

The Mullet or 'Wu Tau' is quite plentiful around Hong Kong and you often come across it being consumed in Thai restaurants on small fish-shaped hot plates. They are very fond of estuarine and harbour environments and like to feed on scraps of rubbish thrown into the water. Sai Kung Harbour is full of shoals of these fish, all of a small 15 cm size, feeding on the scraps thrown into the water from the seafood restaurants. I have not seen too many large Mullet apart from those that exist inside exclusive marinas where people cannot easily fish due to access problems.

Mullet fishing is rather like fishing for river fish in the United Kingdom. You need to make an attractor first, so ground-baiting is necessary. This can be done by either throwing in bread which has been mashed up into crumbs and small lumps along with some fishy-smelling food such as tinned pilchards or by filling up a porous bag or net with the bait so that it gradually filters out into the current flowing past the boat or shoreline. This is called 'burley' or 'chumming' the water and is designed to induce the fish to feed confidently on the stream of food.

An angler should arm himself with a float fishing rod of 11-12ft in length, a thin clear fishing line of 4-6 pounds breaking strain (fluorocarbon) and a small clear plastic float with the shot placed right underneath the float. The hook should be small and about size 14 or 12 and there should be no weights near the hook so that the bait will move naturally in the current. Besides, the fish is highly observant and quickly alerted if it can see the tackle in the water. A piece of bread flake or fish flesh should be lightly squeezed around the hook and after lowering the tackle into the water the float should be allowed to drift along with the current so that the bait travels naturally and wavers slightly in the water.

The fish should be convinced that it is seeing a piece of scrap food passing in front of it so that it will then take the bait. The bite indication can be quite light on the float with only a small dip in the float's movement. If an angler can time his strike correctly, he will suddenly find himself in charge of a very strong fighting fish that will strip line off his reel and provide some exciting action as it attempts to escape.

Once the fish has been brought to the water's edge or next to the boat, a landing net should be used to bring it to dry land as lifting the fish out of the water by the tackle may end up with the hook becoming dislodged from its mouth.

Mullet fishing is not easy and a calm temperament is a prerequisite. Once you have got the feeding right, then the fish will bite with confidence and you can have great sport and perhaps get a good one for dinner.

Mike on Tso Wo Hang Pier with Scooby, his inquisitive Beagle in sleeping mode.

Squid

Squid fishing is very much a 'Sai Kung sport' which commences in May each year and lasts through to September. Each night junks pick up crowds from the piers and head out into Port Shelter where they anchor up and shine bright arc lights into the sea. The lights attract fish and squid who will start patrolling and shoaling around the light beam. Anglers will jig multi-hook lures up and down in the light beam and the squid will attack these.

The secret in catching them is to drop your lure to the sea floor and start jigging up and down at that location and gradually get shallower and shallower. This motion will draw the squid closer to the surface where they will dart in and out trying to catch the lure. Once they are shallow, they are easier to catch and you jig the lure until one attaches its tentacles to the barbs of the hooks. When squid are attached, the angler should raise the squid slowly so as to prevent the tentacles ripping off. Anglers should also watch out for the ink which the squid will normally squirt with great power and accuracy near the surface. The secret is to let the squid squirt at the surface and then bring it onboard for unhooking. At all times remain smooth in handling squid that are attached. Squid rods are generally 'soft' in action for this reason.

Packages for this activity are about HK$190 per person for four hours plus food. Guests going on the boat normally bring drinks, including copious amounts of alcohol, and it is not uncommon for trips to develop a party atmosphere with a bit of fishing to keep it interesting.

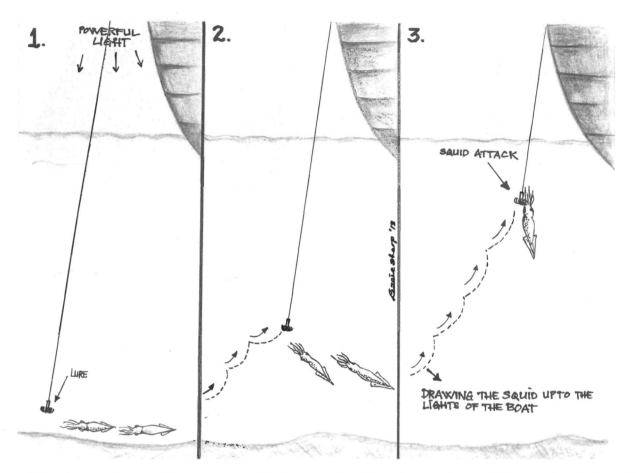

1. POWERFUL LIGHT

LURE

2.

3. SQUID ATTACK

DRAWING THE SQUID UPTO THE LIGHTS OF THE BOAT

The above pictures demonstrate the lure action that draws the squid up to the lights of the boat where they will attack the lure and become snagged on the lure.

These trips are great fun with lots of screaming as people get hosed with squid ink, and cheers when successful catches are made. In addition it is interesting to see what other fish swim into the light beam.

Squid Ink—you should wash it off all surfaces straight away with saltwater before it stains. Squid will normally squirt ink when they surface so anglers should be on guard.

Some anglers take squid fishing very seriously and go to great trouble to catch decent specimens. The general style is to use a soft action or flexible spinning rod and a light fluorocarbon line which is nearly transparent underwater. Fish-shaped lures are cast out next to rocky features or reefs and jigged back to the angler. If fortunate, a squid will attack the lure and become entangled in the points of the hooks. The drag on the reel should be set lightly so as to not break any tentacles off the squid by pulling too hard, and once the squid is attached the angler should gently play it into the water in front of him. Then the squid should either be netted or carefully lifted clear of the water in the hope that it does not detach itself. When specialising in this type of fishing it pays to have a selection of different-coloured lures in case the squid are funny about a particular colour. Anglers should also be careful of the beak of the large squid which can give a very nasty bite if you allow the tentacles to purchase on your hand, so grab them at the tail end.

Jigging lures in the light of the lamps. This attracts both fish and squid and its interesting to see what appears.

Squid Lures showing a fish-like lure on the right and two night lures; one of which will glow if placed under a torch in the first place.

Squid being drawn into the shallow water before landing

Large squid attached to a squid lure cast from a rocky outcrop demonstrating its feelings by changing to a dark red and brown colour.

SPECIES OF FISH CAUGHT AROUND HONG KONG

Fresh Water

Common Carp-Bottom Feeder

Mirror Carp-Bottom Feeder

Big Head Carp-Surface Feeder

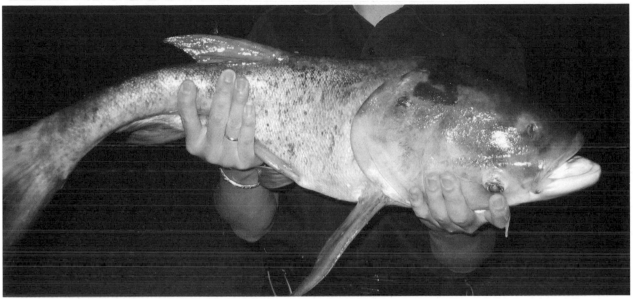

"half blood"

Grass Carp-Surface / Midwater and Bottom Feeder

Indian (Rohu) Carp-Bottom Feeder

knots

"half blood"

"knotless"

Mud Carp-Bottom & Midwater Feeder

Bream-Bottom Feeder

Striped Snakehead-Predatory

Bass (Gwai Far)-Predatory

Freshwater Wrasse-Predatory

88

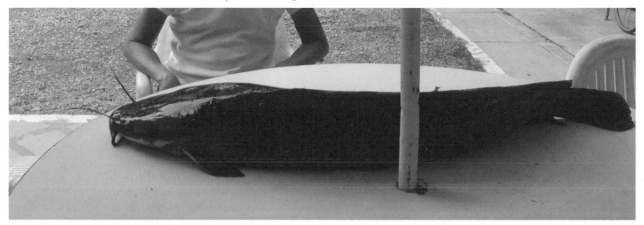

African Catfish-Bottom Feeder

Paul Cowling with a freshly landed catfish.

Tilapia-Bottom & Mid-water Feeder

Pleco-Bottom Feeder

Barb-Bottom / Midwater / Surface Feeder

Salt Water

Red Grouper-Bottom Feeder / Predatory

Lizard Fish-Bottom Feeder / Scavenger

*Areolate Grouper-Bottom Feeder
Scavenger / Predatory*

Sea Bream-Mid-water / Scavengers

Peacock Wrasse-Coral and Rocky Outcrops Scavenger

Puffer Fish-Shallow Water and Rocky areas Scavenger

Asian Barramundi-Mid-water to Surface Feeder / Predatory

Red Snapper
Rocky Outcrops Predatory

Black Bream
Midwater Scavenger

Pomfret
Midwater to Surface Predatory and Scavenger.

HOT RECIPES

Baked Pomfret

Step One

Clean the fish and remove the intestines, gills and scales.

Step Two

Score the fish with 3-4 vertical cuts then sprinkle with lemon or lime juice and salt. Wrap in tin foil and place in preheated oven (375°)or BBQ for 15 minutes.

Step Three

Make the sauce by using:

2 spring onions, sliced, with the green stems sliced as well

1 fresh chilli

3 kaffir lime leaves (cut out the hard stems)

3-4 cloves of minced garlic

1 tbsp lemon/lime juice

2 tbsp fish sauce

4 tbsp olive oil

2 tbsps soy sauce

Then mix the ingredients in a blender.

Step Four

Heat sauce in pan. Place cooked fish in serving dish and pour sauce over the top. Decorate with slices of lemon, fresh basil, cut chilli and sliced spring onion.

Cooking Mussels

It is important when obtaining mussels that you get them from a clean source. Look for shells that are tightly closed. Discard any mussels that have opened when you get them home.

Step One

Rinse the mussels with cold running water. Scrub them with a brush to remove any seaweed, dirt or particles. Remove the stringy beard.

Step Two

Get a wok or large pot and add 2cm of water, white wine (Sauvignon Blanc), some garlic, butter and basil.

Step Three

Bring the pot to a medium heat level and then add the mussels. They should stay in the liquid for 6-8 minutes until the majority of mussels have opened up. It is safe to eat mussels that have not opened up during the cooking phase.

Step Four

Serve in a bowl with some of the sauce and bread. A Tabasco dip goes well with mussels.

Deep Fried Squid

Deep fried squid is a very popular dish amongst Hong Kong seafoodies and is simple to make.

Ingredients:

- 0.5kg of cleaned squid
- One egg yolk
- One cup of ice-cold sparkling water
- 1/8 teaspoon of baking soda
- 1 teaspoon of salt
- ¼ cup of corn starch
- ¾ cup of plain flour
- Canola oil

Step One

Chop the squid into rings and segments. Mix the baking soda, salt, corn starch and flour together. Heat up the oil in a deep pot or deep fryer (6cm deep).

Step Two

Heat the oil until it is boiling at 360 degrees. Take the sparkling water out of the fridge and mix it with the egg yolk. Add all of the other dry ingredients and mix together. Once all is mixed, start adding batches of squid (6-8 pieces) and coating them in the mixture.

Step Three

Drop the batches of squid into the fryer and let them stay there for 45 seconds to a minute. Remove the squid and place them on a paper towel to drain.

Step Four

Serve with soy or seafood sauce with chilli slices added for that extra zing.

Other
DESTINATIONS

The whole point of this book has been to promote fishing in Hong Kong. However, nearby in Southeast Asia there is world-class fishing accessible to the travelling angler. In particular, Thailand has some of the biggest freshwater fish species in the world. Within their waters you can very easily find yourself fighting a 50kg+ fish on tackle normally seen on a deep-sea fishing boat due to the power of these species.

Thailand

Thailand's fame in the fishing world began when TV networks such as Discovery, National Geographic and BBC sent their angling celebrities and naturalists over to the country to do battle with the Giant Mekongs and Siamese Carp and this placed the country into mainstream fishing media. The great thing is that many of the famous locations are easily accessible from Bangkok and many of the tour operators will pick you up from your hotel and provide transport, guides, tackle and lunch.

The major species targeted in Thailand fall into two categories. Firstly there are the native species: Mekong Catfish, Striped Catfish, Chao Phraya Catfish, Rohu Carp, Siamese Carp, Jungle Barb, Giant Snakehead and Giant Stingray being the most famous. Secondly there are the imported species, which are now bred locally and stocked into lakes and ponds. These are generally Amazonian with the most popular being Arapaima, Tiger Catfish, Red Tail Catfish, Pacu and Peacock Bass.

Of course, those locations holding the biggest stock fish charge the most, especially since

Arapaima are not good survivors after being caught by anglers and need a lot of careful handling in order that they can swim away safely after capture. The more Amazonian species available to target in a location the more the fishing will cost (approaching 7,000 baht a day) so we have provided a selection of locations and companies that can provide you the best choice.

Company: Fish Thailand

www.fishthailand.co.uk

This UK company has been employed by both the BBC and Discovery Channel and remains one of the most professional and enthusiastic operations in Thailand. They have their own well stocked water at Jurassic Mountain Resort Fishing Park, which is very good.

Location: Cha-Am Fishing Park

www.cha-amfishing-resort.com

This is a good locally managed fishing park located outside Cha Am. There are two ponds available (carp/catfish or predator) and a day- ticket for the carp/catfish water is only 200 baht a day. However, the predator pond costs more as the fish are mainly Amazonian. Accommodation and restaurant available.

Mike with a 25 pound Indian Rohu Carp caught at Kau Luem Dam from a fishing raft. This reservoir is located up next to the border with Myanmar.

Location: Pilot III

This is a spinning and fly-fishing park. It is especially good for Barramundi and Giant Snakehead. It is located off the Bangna-Trad Highway near Bangkok. The day tickets are very reasonable.

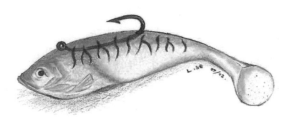

Location: Bungsamran Fishing Park

www.bungsamran.com

This fishing park is world-famous and appears regularly on fishing programmes. It contains huge fish including some world record sized species and the assistance of a guide is advisable. The current prices are 1,000 baht per rod per day, a local Thai guide is 1,000 baht per day and the renting of a rod/reel plus tackle is 500 baht per session with a 1,000 baht deposit. If a company is hired then the cost is much more however, their service makes the day a lot better with all matters i.e. transport, guides, equipment, taken care of.

Christian Sharp pictured with a 30 pound Striped Catfish along with Ali ; who is one of Fish Thailand's guides at Bungsamran.

Large Tilapia caught with Eddie Mounce that was destined for the local fisherman's pot.

7Kg Barramundi caught at Boon Mar Ponds, Nr. Bangkok.

Mike with a 25Kg Siamese Carp caught at Shadow Lake in Bangkok

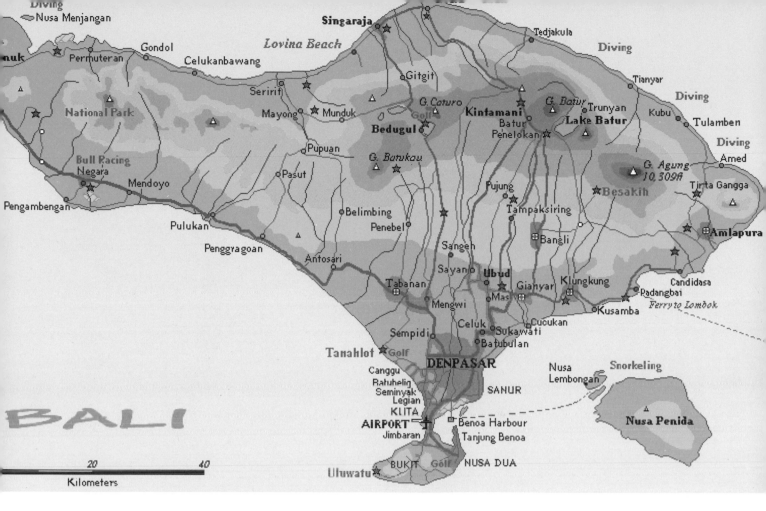

Bali, Indonesia

Sport-fishing in Bali is different from Thailand in that there is a greater emphasis on saltwater bottom and game-fishing. Around Sanur are some freshwater ponds with catfish, barramundi and milkfish but not on the same scale as Thailand. Even so, should you wish to fish while staying in Bali then the following company is good - though expensive - when it comes to sea fishing.

Company: Ena Dive Centre and Marine Adventures

www.enafishing.com

Located in Sanur, South East Bali.

This is a large operation that covers both fishing and diving. The fishing is not cheap

however, they do offer a wide spectrum of fishing activities along with guides and boats and you will catch fish

If these destinations don't provide enough activity then simply get onto the internet and look up freshwater fishing in India, game fishing in Micronesia or simply get down to Australia and you will find what you are looking for.

Bottom fishing off Sanur Reef, in Bali.

APPENDIX

Glossary of Commonly Used Fishing Terms

Algae:	Plant organisms found in ponds, lakes and reservoirs.
Angler:	Someone who hunts or pursues fish with a rod and line or pole in freshwater or saltwater environments.
Angling:	The sport of hunting fish with a rod and line.
Artificial Baits:	Baits fashioned out of wood, plastic and other materials and intended to imitate the natural equivalent.
Attractor:	Baits or samples of the bait that are used to attract fish to the angler.
Backing Line:	Fishing line or braid wound onto a spool to provide more range to the line or fill out a fishing reel.
Bagging Up:	UK term for catching a lot of fish and keeping them in a net.
Bail Arm:	Arm on a fishing reel that either restricts or frees the flow of line. It also acts as a line guide.
Bait:	Natural item such as worm, sweet corn, bread or fish and others which are used to induce fish to try to eat what the angler is using on his hook.
Bait Fish:	Small fish or fry that often provide food for bigger fish.
Bait Needle:	Long needle with a small hook at the end used for attaching bait to hook or line. Used in conjunction with a hair rig.
Bait Runner:	Type of fitting to a Fixed Spool Reel that allows a fish to take line from the reel. Once the angler engages the drag by turning the handle, the reel will wind in line and give line depending on the strength of the fish.
Barb:	The point on the end of a hook that secures it in a fish's mouth. It is very common for anglers to remove these to make it easier to unhook fish.
Bead:	Small rubber balls with holes through the middle that are placed on fishing line between weights and swivels to act as a shock absorber
Bite/Biting:	When a fish takes the bait on a hook. When fish keep trying to eat the bait on a hook they are 'biting'.
Boom:	Length of metal or plastic used to separate hook and line from the main line. Technical term- 'Paternoster'. Prevents tangling.

Bottom Feeder:	Fish species that predominantly feed off food on the bottom of the lake, river or sea bed.
Bottom Fishing:	Placing your bait on the bottom of the lake river or sea bed to catch bottom feeders.
Breaking Strain:	Measurement used to identify strengths of line. Example; 10 Pound line will break if pulled to a strength over 10 pounds.
Butt Pad:	Often nicknamed the 'mangina'. This is a padded cup an angler wears over his groin in order to place the butt of the rod in when he is playing a large fish.
Casting:	When an angler throws his line and bait out onto the water he is casting.
Catch and Release:	Common practice that anglers use to preserve stocks by releasing their fish once they have been brought to the bank or boat.
Chum:	Chopped and mashed up bait, normally rotting fish and offal that is added to sea water in order to attract types of fish to come near the anglers. Australian term; 'burley'.
Coarse Fishing:	Angling for all freshwater fish species apart from those considered as 'Game Fish' such as Trout, Salmon or Bass.
Dead bait:	When a dead fish or prawn is tied to a hook in order to tempt predators. Using a dead bait is called 'dead baiting'.
Disgorger:	Small tool used to remove hooks trapped inside a fish's mouth.
Drift Fishing:	Fishing from a boat that is drifting with the wind and current.
Drop Off.	A sudden change in depth underwater such as a cliff.
Dry Fly:	An artificial fly tied onto a hook that is presented onto the surface of the water.
Ebb-Tide:	Tide going out or a falling tide.
Estuary:	Where a river flows into the sea and normally where fish will spawn and home to schools of juvenile fish.
Fathom:	Old measurement used by seamen to measure depth. (1 Fathom = 6 feet.)

Feeder:	Small cage or coil attached to the line near the hook and used to introduce more bait to the area where the hook is lying.
Feeding-on-the-top:	When fish feed off the surface of the water.
Fixed Spool Reel:	Common type of reel that can allow an angler to cast easily by releasing the bail arm.
Floater:	Bait that is floating on the water surface such as bread or dog biscuits.
Fluorocarbon:	High quality fishing line that is opaque and is near-transparent underwater.
Forceps:	Medical tool adopted by anglers as a useful tool for removing fish hooks from fish mouths.
Fry:	Small juvenile fish.
Game Fish:	Sporting fish such as Trout, Salmon, Marlin, Tuna etc.
Ground bait:	Samples of the hook bait thrown into the area where an angler is fishing in order to attract fish to feed there.
Hair Rig:	A piece of line attached to a hook in order to trick a nervous fish into tasting the bait without detecting the hook. Normally used for carp fishing.
Hemp:	A popular type of seed used for ground baiting. Its smell is very effective in encouraging fish to feed.
Hook:	A shaped piece of wire that is sharpened at one end so that it catches a fish's mouth if a fish bites. Large fish need large hooks small fish need small hooks and shy fish will need a smaller hook than normally used.
Hook Length:	A piece of line attached to the hook. Together they are called the 'trace'
IGFA:	Florida based organization called the International Game Fish Association that records large fish and line strengths. An 'IGFA Record Fish' is one caught on particular line strength.
Inshore-Fishing	Fishing from a boat near the shore or estuary.
Jig:	Metallic fish with a hook attached moved up and down below a boat which attracts fish to take it, thinking it is a real fish.
Jigging:	Using a jig as explained above.

Landing Net:	Net used to get fish that an angler has brought to the bank onto the bank. Prevents any breakage when the fish is brought out of the water.
Leader:	The length of fishing line between thick fly fishing line and the fly. Can be tapered.
Ledger: (Ledgering)	Fishing with a lead weight on the bottom of a lake, river or a seabed. See Bottom Fishing.
Line Bite:	Where a fish accidentally swims into the fishing line giving a false bite indication. Often a sign fish are interested in your bait.
Live Bait:	When a live fish or prawn is placed on a hook so that it remains alive and swims around.
Mainline:	The main line wound onto a fishing reel. 150-250 metres or even longer when targeting large game fish.
Match Fishing:	Competitive fishing between anglers. Normally the angler with the greatest weight of fish wins the match
Method Feeder:	Large feeder designed to introduce ground bait to where the hook is placed.
Monofilament line:	Plastic type of line with set breaking strains 1 pound to 100 pound breaking-strain. The line is stretchy as opposed to Braided Line which does not stretch.
Multiplier:	Sea fishing reel that allows the spool to turn 5-6 revolutions to one turn of the handle.
Neap Tide:	The tide with the least difference or movement between high or low water. Happens during the first and last quarter of the moon
Nymph:	Artificial bait used to imitate the stage of a flies development when it inhabits the water environment as a crawler or predatory bug.
Offshore fishing:	Fishing some distance from the coastline in deep-water
Outrigger:	Large boom placed on a boat to allow a trolling bait to be towed clear of the boat and other lines.
Particles:	Refers to types of bait such as sweet corn, nuts, hemp and dried beans etc.
Peg:	An allotted position on a freshwater facility given to match fishermen. Normally drawn from a bag in order to be fare as some pegs are known to be better than others.
Playing:	After an angler hooks a fish, the fish will attempt to escape and an angler will have to give and take line until the fish is exhausted.

Plug:	Wooden or plastic artificial lure that resembles an injured fish. Predators will attack the plug as it is pulled through the water.
Plumbing-the-depth:	A large weight is attached to the hook so that the angler can adjust his float tackle so as to put the hook on the bottom.
Plummet:	The weight used for plumbing-the-depth.
Pole-Fishing:	Pole fishing means the line is attached to the end of the fibre- glass or carbon-fibre pole. There is no reel. UK poles have elastics attached between the line and the pole to allow for large fish to be played.
Priest:	Term used for the heavy object used to dispatch fish before they are taken home to eat.
Pumping:	When a large fish is being played, an angler retrieves line by hauling on the rod and then winding the slack. This is called 'pumping'
Quiver-Tip:	Type of rod with a more sensitive tip that indicates a bite by curving round.
Reel:	The fishing reel is an essential piece of equipment that holds line and casts line when required. Types: Fixed-Spool, Multiplier, Centre-Pin and Closed Face.
Re-Stocking:	Replacing farm bred fish into a freshwater environment.
Rig:	The terminal tackle upon which the bait is attached.
Rise:	When a fish swims up to the surface and grabs a fly or nymph. Normally leaves a circular ripple.
Rod-rest:	Tool upon which you rest the rod while fishing.
Run:	During the playing of a fish it will attempt to swim away at speed, this is called a 'run'.
Setting-the-hook:	When an angler strikes or applies tension to the line causing the hook to catch the fishes' mouth.
Shot (Split-shot):	Small metal weights that are split to allow them to be squeezed onto the line. Normally given sizes such as BB, 2BB etc.
Sinking Fly-line:	Flyline that after you have cast will sink underwater. Used for lures and wet flies.
Slack-Tide:	Short period between the ebb and flood tides when current is at its weakest.

Spin:	Action of casting a metal or wooden lure and retrieving it so that a predatory fish believes that it is a bait fish or injured fish.
Spool:	On a Fixed-Spool fishing reel, the spool will hold the line. Anglers will have 2-3 spools holding different line strengths.
Stick Float:	A straight float, normally used in rivers, that are attached to the line by either shot or rubbers and are sometimes referred to as 'Wagglers'.
Strike:	When fish takes a bait, the angler will lift the rod and strike into the fish by jerking action thereby setting the hook.
Surfcaster:	An angler that fishes in the surf.
Swimfeeder:	Small porous container attached to mainline designed to place some feed in the area of your hook bait.
Swivel.	Important piece of kit that lies between mainline and traces thereby preventing tangles and twists.
Test Curve:	Measurement used to define how strong a rod is. The measurement refers to the amount of weight used to bend the rod through 90 degrees.
Terminal Tackle:	Similar to 'rig' and means the tackle used at the working end and includes hook, weight and swivels etc.
Trace:	The length of line attached to the hook. If dealing with predators, a wire trace is sometimes used to preventing the fish biting through the line.
Treble Hook:	A hook which has three points.
Troll:	To pull a dead-bait or lure from behind a boat which is underway at no more than 6 knots
Trolling:	The action when you troll.
Watercraft:	The craft of an angler where he reads the water conditions and decides where and how he shall fish.

English-Chinese Dictionary

You may find this section useful when out fishing in Hong Kong.

Fishing Equipment and Baits

Artificial Baits	假餌
Attractor	誘餌
Backing Line	後備絲
Bail Arm	線擋
Bait	餌
Bait Fish	小魚餌
Bait Needle	餌針
Barb	倒鈎
Bead	擋珠
Chum	撒餌
Dead Bait	死餌
Disgorger	脫鈎器
Feeder	誘餌籠
Fixed Spool Reel	直絞 (紡車式捲線器)
Floater	浮餌
Fluorocarbon	碳纖絲
Fly (Fly-fishing)	毛鈎
Forceps	鑷子
Ground Bait	撒餌
Grub	蛆蟲
Hook	魚鈎
Hook Length	子線
Jig	路亞餌
Krill	南極蝦 (磷蝦)
Landing Net	手撈網 (撈箕)
Live Bait	生餌
Mainline	主線
Monofilament Line	單絲纖維
Multiplier	雙軸捲線器
Needle-Float	浮針
Nymph	飛蠅擬餌
Outrigger	舷外托架
Paste	粉餌
Plug	小魚形擬餌
Plummet	沉子 (鉛錘)
Quiver-Tip	顫動竿梢
Ragworm	沙蟲

Reel	捲絲器 (絞)
Rig	釣組
Rod	魚竿
Rod-rest	竿架
Shot (Split-shot)	夾鉛
Shrimp	蝦
Sinking Fly-line	沉水線
Spool	線軸 (線杯)
Stick-float	長浮標
Surface Boppers	浮標
Sweetcorn	玉米粒
Swivel	撐圈
Treble Hook	三爪鈎

Species Names

Amberjack	章雄 (高體鰤)
Areolate Grouper	芝麻斑
Arowana	龍魚
Barb	七星魚 (花鯽)
Barracuda	竹簽 (海狼)
Barramundi	盲鰽
Big Head Carp	大魚 (大頭魚)
Black Bream	黑鮊 (黑沙鮊)
Black Marlin	旗魚
Bluefin Tuna	藍鰭吞拿魚
Bream	鯛魚
Brown Marbled Grouper	老虎斑
Catfish	庵釘(赤魚)
Chinese Mackerel (Chinese Seerfish)	青鮫 (牛皮鮫)
Clam	蜆
Cobia	憕仔魚 (魚仲)
Common Carp	鯉魚
Dorado	牛頭魚 (鬼頭刀)
Eel	鱔 (鰻)
Garfish	雀鱔
Giant Trevally	大魚仔
Goldfish	鯽鱼 (鯽魚)
Grass Carp	鯇魚 (草魚)
Grouper	石斑
Gwai Far (Mandarin Fish)	桂花魚 (鱖魚)

Kawa Kawa Tuna	巴鰹	Red Drum	星鱸 (紅鼓)
Lizard Fish	狗棍	Red Grouper	紅斑
Marlin	旗魚 (馬林魚)	Red Snapper	紅魚
Mirror Carp	鏡鯉 (三道鱗)	Rohu	南亞野鯪 (露斯塔野鯪)
Moray Eels	花鰡 (泥婆)	Sailfish	旗魚
Mud Carp	鯪魚	Silver Carp	鯿魚
Mullet	鰽魚	Squid	魷魚
Mussel	青口	Snakehead	生魚 (鱧魚)
Peacock Wrasse	花鰭海豬魚	Snapper	鯛魚
Pipe Fish	尖嘴魚	Sprat	小鯡魚
Pleco	清道夫 (琵琶魚)	Striped Snakehead	線鱧
Pomfret	鯧魚 (鱠魚)	Tilapia	金山鯽 (非洲鯽)
Prawn	大蝦	Tuna	吞拿魚
Puffer Fish	雞泡魚 (河豚)	Wahoo	竹鮫
Rabbit Fish	泥鯭	Wrasse	隆頭魚
Rainbow Runner	雙帶鰺	Wu Tau (Grey Mullet)	烏頭
Ray	魔鬼魚	Yellow Fin Tuna	黃鰭杜仲

Useful Resources in Hong Kong

Category	Name	Address	Contact Details
Fishing Permit (All Reservoirs)	Water Supplies Department Valid 1st Sept to 31st Mar Cost: HK$28	Wanchai Customer Enq. Ctr 1/F Immigration Tower, 7 Gloucester Road, Wanchai, Hong Kong 📁✉ Mongkok Customer Enq. Ctr G/F 128 Sai Yee Street, Mongkok, Kowloon	28294799 / 28294559
Fishing Ponds	Duck Fishing Pond	Nim Wan Road, Lau Fau Shan, Yuen Long, N.T.	24726134 www.yl.hk/duck
	Ho Jie	Nim Wan Road, Lau Fau Shan, Yuen Long, N.T.	24723508 www.yl.hk/hofish
	Luk Keng	Luk Keng, Brides Pool Road, Sha Tau Kok, N.T.	
	Go Go	Tung Tsz, Ting Kok Road, Tai Po, N.T.	
	Sheung Pak Ngai Fishing Pond	Nim Wan Road, Lau Fau Shan, Yuen Long, N.T.	
Big Game Fishing	Tailchasers (Hong Kong fishing)	Main Office, Shum Wan Road, Aberdeen, H.K.	91220695 www.hongkongfishing.com hongkongfishing@gmail.com
	Thai Lady Sport Fishing	-	90277948 www.thailadysportfishing.com carmine@hkconnection.com
Squid Fishing	Jubilee		35555555 www.jubilee.com.hk

Tackle Shops	Po Kee Fishing Tackle Co. Ltd	6 Hillier Street, Sheung Wan, H.K.	25441035
	Lun Shing Fishing Shop	1/F Shui On Court, 1-3 Tai Yuen Street, (Rear Lane), Wanchai, H.K.	25728126
	World Fishing Centre	G/F Mido Apartment, 330-332 King's Road, North Point, H.K.	25666306
	World Fishing Centre	G/F Ho Kwan Building, 54 Jordan Road, Kowloon	23020078
	Triton Fishing Equipment Co.	1/F Anton Building, 1 Anton Street, Wanchai, H.K.	28668551
	Triton Fishing Equipment Co.	Shop B, G/F, 4 Ferry Street, Jordan, Kowloon	23887229
	Triton Fishing Equipment Co.	Shop D, 1/F, Fok On Court, 100-108 Ma Tau Chung Rd, Kowloon	27650832
	Hong Kong Sun Wah Fishing Tackle Trading Company (Shimano)	G/F 37 Battery Street, Yau Ma Tei, Kowloon	23844799
	Fishing-One Tackle Shop	Shop 3 Yen Yin Mansion, 8 Ferry Street, Jordan, Kowloon	23856811
	Yat Fan Fung Shun Co	G/F 71 Ho Pui Street, Tsuen Wan, N.T.	24099887 / 24922777 yffsco@fishingtackle.com.hk
	Wai Kee Fishing Tackle Shop	19 Kam Fai Path, Yuen Long, N.T.	24763265
Facebook Sites	<ul><li>Hong Kong Sport Fishing Association</li><li>Hong Kong Fishing with Tailchasers</li><li>Hong Kong Fishing Enthusiasts</li><li>Hong Kong Fishing</li><li>Hong Kong Light Game Fishing</li><li>Hong Kong Fishingendless</li><li>Fishing HK</li><li>Fly Fishing Hong Kong</li></ul>		

Acknowledgements

In producing this fishing guide we would like to express our heartfelt thanks to the following people. Firstly, my wife Lizzie Sharp-Eliazar for her wonderful artwork. I spent hours trying to produce good sketches to no avail and realised the advantage of having a professionally trained artist in the family who could produce first-class work in a very short time.

Secondly, we are very grateful to those anglers and companies that contributed photographs, namely the Au-Yeung family at Tai Mei Tuk, Kim Stuart at Tailchasers and Latvian angler Alex Strelets Strele, as well as Police Sergeant Kent Tong who lent us a very nice camera to use on the book.

Given that this is the first time any of us have worked on a book, we have had to seek advice from professionals in the shape of John Church and Chris Davis, both well known Hong Kong-based writers whose input (generally over a beer or two) has been material in raising the standard of our script to something more acceptable to the publishing world.

In addition, we are grateful to those anglers who provided advice on venues and methods, notably Paul Cowling and Terry Greene.

Finally, a great thank you to our respective family members and partners for putting up with our disappearances at weekends on various fishing expeditions. I suppose if both myself and John were not anglers we would be golfers, as both sports totally absorb the enthusiast to the extent that everything else fades into the background.

About the Authors

Mike Sharp

Born in Berkshire, Mike Sharp started fishing at the age of 12 on and around the River Kennet and its tributaries. He maintained his hobby until he was 18 when work and service life took over. Following a nine-year stint with the British Army (Duke of Edinburgh's Royal Regiment) Mike left the services and joined the then-Royal Hong Kong Police Force in 1991. At this stage he was a seriously keen diver and it was not until 2004 that he returned to fishing as his main interest. Mike has fished in the UK, Canada, Australia, Indonesia, Brunei, Thailand as well as extensively in Hong Kong. He is married to Lizzie and serves as a Chief Inspector in the Hong Kong Police. When John returns to Hong Kong, it is very common to find both of them spending their weekends beside Hong Kong's many ponds and lakes.

John Peters

Born in Essex to a farming family, John Peters can truly be called a globe-trotting angler. He first picked up a rod at the age of five and quickly progressed to specimen hunting in his teens. During his twenties, John explored fishing in Mississippi and Florida before moving to Kenya where he spent six years working in the big game fishing industry based out of Mombasa. John routinely returns to his farm in Essex and participates in the local match fishing scene with some notable successes – as the contents of his glass cabinets demonstrate. In 2009, John started visiting Hong Kong and quickly teamed up with Mike Sharp to explore the Hong Kong and Thai fishing destinations. His experience and know-how have been material to the creation of this book. John lives in Chelmsford but annually visits Hong Kong for more fishing adventures with Mike.

The Illustrator

Lizzie Sharp-Eliazar

Born in Jakarta to a Dutch-Indonesian trading family, Lizzie attended one of the city's most prestigious girls' schools (Tarakanita I) before going on to qualify as a professional fashion designer at Sonsbeek Mode en Kleding School in the Netherlands. Lizzie has covered several different career paths, starting out as an ambassador's secretary for the Embassy of Brazil, fashion model, flight attendant for Cathay Pacific Airways, freelance fashion designer, Customer Services Manager for Animal Hospital and a playgroup teacher for ESF Hong Kong. Unlike her husband Mike, Lizzie has no angling interest and remains focused on drawing and designing as her main pastime. Her illustrations are spread throughout the book as are some of her great photographs. She lives with Mike in Sai Kung, along with three dogs and a large amount of fishing tackle.

EXPLORE ASIA WITH BLACKSMITH BOOKS

From retailers around the world or from *www.blacksmithbooks.com*